*The Bourgeoisie*
*in 18th Century France*

# The Bourgeoisie
# in 18th Century France

BY ELINOR G. BARBER

PRINCETON, NEW JERSEY

PRINCETON UNIVERSITY PRESS

L.C. CARD: 55-10680

ISBN 0-691-02801-X (paperback edn.)

ISBN 0-691-09309-1 (hardcover edn.)

Fourth Printing 1973

Printed in the United States of America
by Princeton University Press, Princeton, New Jersey

*To Bernard*

# Preface

THE purpose of this study of the French bourgeoisie in the 18th century is a dual one: to illuminate, first of all, the position of the bourgeois group in the class structure of French society in that period, and, secondly, to carry out the first aim in a way that will demonstrate the usefulness of a certain kind of social theory in historical research.

As regards the position of the bourgeoisie in France of the *ancien régime*, we shall explore the attitudes of the bourgeois class toward the fundamental values and institutions of the society, and especially toward the class structure, in the hope of clarifying the extent to which these attitudes were, in fact, "revolutionary." Was the bourgeoisie relatively content, or was it dissatisfied with its lot in the society? To what extent were its attitudes overtly and explicitly sympathetic toward a revolution? and to what extent were revolutionary sympathies latent and implicit? In the course of the 18th century, there were significant shifts in the relative power and prestige of the king, the nobility and the bourgeoisie, and we shall attempt to determine the impact of these historical changes on the attitudes of the bourgeois class. These are the kinds of questions we shall try to deal with in the course of our investigation. The answers, tentative, to be sure, emerged gradually out of the evidence of bourgeois actions and bourgeois opinions—they were, generally, not anticipated at the start of our researches.

As regards the usefulness of social theory, the historian is rightly skeptical of the relevance to his subject matter of grand theories dealing with society in general. But these are not what concern us here. Rather, there are also available to the historian what Robert K. Merton has called "theories of the middle range," which attempt to analyze and to relate to one another the different component structures of concrete societies. The theory of social stratification which is used in this study (it is expounded briefly in Chapter I), deals with subject matter entirely familiar to historians, but in a somewhat different way. It is the advantage of this new way that it gives us, we think, new insights into familiar materials and familiar problems.

The principal sources of the sociological theory used in the study of the 18th century French bourgeoisie are the writings of Talcott Parsons and Robert K. Merton.[1] It is to their work that the author is chiefly indebted both for instruction in the nature and use of theory in general, and for useful theory about social stratification in particular.

In studying the class position of the French bourgeoisie of the *ancien régime*, we believe it is primarily desirable to examine the writings of that group itself, in order to see how it assessed its social situation. Unfortunately, the "ordinary" French bourgeois at that time was not much concerned with chronicling and commenting on his experience, and it is just this 18th century bourgeois man-in-the-street whom we are trying to reach. Still, we found some useful memoirs and journals, and some interesting discussions of contemporary institutions by men who were not professional writers, and therefore not self-conscious critics of the society. These are supplemented by the works of the professional writers, including some plays and novels which often make significant unintentional and incidental revelations in their plots.

Two kinds of primary material especially, however, were not available for this study. First, we did not have access to archival material on important problems—for example, on the issuing of letters of nobility, or on the number of the military commissions granted to *roturiers*. Second, and probably counting for less, we could find almost no *livres de raison*, in which

---

[1] Talcott Parsons, *Essays in Sociological Theory, Pure and Applied* (Glencoe, Illinois, 1948), and Robert K. Merton, *Social Theory and Social Structure* (Glencoe, Illinois, 1949).

were recorded the most important domestic events of French family life. Records of dowries and of funeral expenses, for instance, would provide valuable clues to the mobility of bourgeois families. Only a few scattered *livres de raison* could be found reprinted; they do not amount to very much by way of evidence, though from a large number of them it would be possible to make useful generalizations.

In all but a few cases we have followed the example of Daniel Mornet (in *Les origines intellectuelles de la Révolution Française*) and have used only material antedating the period when the Revolution had become an actuality. After 1789 (or even 1787), criticism of previously existing institutions was socially approved by the greater part of the population, and the ambivalences that were latent before were polarized into either complete rejection or the defense unto death of those institutions. Furthermore, revolutionary ardor distorted the memory of many a writer about his earlier attitudes toward society.

As far as the accounts of "objective" observers of the bourgeoisie are concerned, we have depended for an evaluation of the bourgeoisie's social status for the most part on secondary historical works rather than on the writings of the contemporary nobility. The very limited objectivity of the latter group diminishes the value of their observations for a study of the bourgeoisie, except insofar as noble attitudes reacted upon bourgeois aspirations. As for the work of secondary authorities on our subject, we found that the 19th and 20th century historian must often be read in ways he did not anticipate, if his material is to be useful for our purpose. We have gleaned many useful scraps of evidence from biographies, from local histories, and from social, economic, and intellectual history, frequently by authors who had little interest in an analysis of class structure as we understand it.

Just as the aim of this study is in part historical, in part sociological, so also the author's debts are to scholars in the

fields of history and of sociology. For his very generous and
friendly help in the writing of the dissertation on which this
book is based I have a great debt to Professor Crane Brinton
of Harvard University, and I should like to express my grati-
tude. And I am happy to thank my husband, Bernard Barber,
for introducing me to the sociological approach which made
this study possible, as well as for the moral support to which
it owes its completion. At various stages my manuscript was
read and helpfully criticized by the following scholars and
friends, and to all of them I am beholden: Sidney A. Burrell,
Elizabeth Eisenstein, Ruth Emery, J. Jean Hecht, Harry
M. Johnson, David Landes, Jane E. Ruby, and Sylvia L.
Thrupp.

ELINOR G. BARBER

*December 15, 1954*

# *Contents*

*The Bourgeoisie*
*in 18th Century France*

# CHAPTER I

## The Class Structure of 18th Century France

THE society of 18th century France could best be understood by a comprehensive study of all its major social structures: political and economic, kinship, class, and religious. Such a study, too, would take up the relationships of all these structures. The more limited goal of the present study is to focus only on the class (or stratificational) structure of France in this period, and to show, wherever possible, its relations to the other major institutional patterns. Though of necessity this focus highlights the functions of the class structure, it should not be mistaken for the allocation of greater significance to that one part as compared to the other parts of the society.

### Introductory: A Brief Sketch of a Functional Theory of Social Stratification

For the successful functioning of any social system that is at all highly differentiated, some system of stratification is necessary. (Other such functional systems are the structures mentioned above, political, religious, economic, etc.) The stratification system integrates the evaluations of people that are made in a society, and thus it provides the regularity and stability of expectation that is essential to all social action. People must know what degree of respect or condescension to expect from or mete out to their fellows, and the criteria of evaluation on which the stratification hierarchy is based give them the appropriate orientation. Whatever the standards are according to which people are differentially evaluated in any given society, there must be widespread consensus among its members both about these standards themselves and about the "proper" treatment of people in terms of these standards.

The criteria according to which people are evaluated fall into the same basic categories in all societies, because they are closely related to the functional needs of *any* going society. The *emphasis* on the different criteria varies, however, with the needs of different societies and with the values of the society in which the criteria are applied. The universal criteria of evaluation and differentiation are derived from the relative skill and responsibility with which individuals perform the following kinds of important social roles: property roles, political roles, religious roles, and occupational roles. However, feudal society emphasized skill and responsibility in religious, political, and military roles, while modern industrial society emphasizes competence in business and professional roles.

Social classes exist within a stratification hierarchy insofar as the members of groups of families treat each other as equal in status. The evidence for the existence of such social classes lies fairly close to the surface of social behavior, although it is very hard to measure with any accuracy, for difference and equality of status among people are expressed in the form of the degree of intimacy of their social relations. First in order of importance as such an expression of equality is courtship and marriage; and there are many lesser forms of intimate social relations, such as dining together. Furthermore, members of a given social class will conform to a certain style of life to symbolize their status. They will choose only certain occupations, live in certain kinds of homes, and dress or speak in a particular way. Members of the society use these symbols to place one another, but while in some societies certain key symbols alone may be taken as conclusive evidence of a certain class status, in other societies it may require several symbols to piece together such an identification.

Societies vary not only in the different emphasis given by their functional needs and their values to the criteria of evaluation but in the rigidity with which social class lines are maintained. This degree of rigidity will depend on the approved attitudes in a given society toward social mobility, that is, toward the movement of individuals from the social class they occupy at birth into another class, either higher or lower in the hierarchy of classes. Attitudes toward social mobility vary from approval of complete equality of opportunity at one end of the scale, to the complete prohibition of any change in status at the other end. This range of approved attitudes makes it possible to construct a typology of stratification systems. The polar types on the continuum, the extremes of which we have indicated above, have been called the open class system and the caste system; the former is found in its most highly developed form in the United States, the latter in India.

In the caste society, there is strong moral disapproval of social mobility, so that the status of the individual is ascribed to him by the status of the family into which he is born, and it is henceforth immutable. The various social roles, prestigious and non-prestigious alike, remain in the same families from generation to generation. Intermarriage between members of different castes is strictly prohibited, as are also other social relations, and in the extreme case, even physical contact. The other polar type of stratification system, the open class system, is, of course, more familiar to Americans. Since, in this type, mobility is strongly institutionalized, i.e., given moral approval, it is the relative ability of individuals that will determine their accession to prestigious or non-prestigious roles. Ideally, family origin is irrelevant to adult status, and in fact it can give, at most, differential opportunity toward its achievement, for social roles are allocated on the basis of skill and competence. High political authority and great wealth, for example, are accessible to anyone. Neither in India nor in the United States is the ideal-typical caste or open class system realized, for no concrete society can ever achieve this, but these two societies probably come closest to a concrete realization of the polar types.

Between the poles of the continuum there is a wide variety of mixtures of the two ideal types, mixtures in which one or the other of the two patterns predominates. Any concrete society, as we suggested above, is necessarily constituted, to a certain degree, of patterns deriving from both the caste and the open class types. The complete approval of mobility is incompatible with strong moral sentiments about family ties, and in the caste system allowance must be made for the undeniable claims of unusual talent. But over and beyond these fundamental conflicts, there is a wide variation in the predominance of one set of patterns over the other, and near the midpoint of the continuum they may come into an uneasy balance. Near this mid-point, secondary patterns win considerable approval, and in some cases legal sanction. Rigid class endogamy, as enforced by the caste system, may break down here, as does any clearly defined hierarchy of socially prestigious roles, and the appropriate way of life of any individual cannot be defined either by the social importance of his role alone, or, simply, by his family connections. We shall see presently that 18th century French society represents such a mixture of types as we have briefly described. This mixture has sometimes been called an "Estate society," but the term is not very useful, and leads to unnecessary confusion with the political and legal systems of the society.

Since the caste system and the open class system are based on fundamentally different and indeed contradictory social values, a stratification system in which both these types are represented may impose some strain on the members of the society. The two principal value complexes involved in such conflicts are those of universalism and particularism. The first confers the moral obligation to give all men an equal initial chance, and to reward competence and recognize achievement. The second gives primary value to the individual's loyalties to the members of a particular group, whether it be a kin or local group, regardless of competence. Compromises between the two can never be made without some strain and without the violation of many people's sense of justice, though these compromises need not be seriously dysfunctional to the total society.

The present study will be chiefly concerned with examining the consequences of the mixture of caste and open class patterns of stratification in 18th century French society for one large class in that society, namely for the bourgeoisie.

### *The Class Structure and the Revolution of 1789*

The composite stratification system of 18th century France came out of three distinct historical traditions. First, the medieval-feudal tradition brought the primary emphasis on the criteria of political authority and property and of a military career. Also, it brought considerable though not complete disapproval of social mobility: the importance of physical prowess in military combat had necessitated some allowance for personal competence in the formation and development of the knightly class, though this margin for competence diminished and the class rigidified in the course of the Middle Ages. Broadly speaking, the feudal tradition institutionalized a caste system, and the individual's status was ascribed to him depending on his birth into one or the other of the following two groups: the *noble*—that which at one time had held political authority on the basis of property in land, and both of these as a reward for military aid to the king; and the *non-noble*—that which had had no such authority or property and which had the lowly occupational role of tilling the soil. Medieval Catholic ideology was largely congruent with the prevalent institutional definition of the social hierarchy. In the great and tragic social cleavages that it conceived between the rich and the poor, the powerful and the humble, there was no place for the bourgeoisie, the "middle class."[1] And from the point of view of the social teachings of the Catholic Church about order in society, bourgeois social mobility was tantamount to a direct challenge to the existing, divinely appointed order.[2]

[1] Bernhard Groethuysen, *Die Entstehung der Buergerlichen Welt- und Lebensanschauung in Frankreich* (Halle, 1930), II, p. 10.

[2] *Ibid.*, pp. 199-200.

By the 18th century, membership in a noble family still carried high prestige, even though the property and the political authority of the family might have dwindled considerably by that time. High religious authority was likewise prestigious from feudal times, especially since it too was connected with political authority and landed property, and though it was obviously not hereditary in the same way as political authority, nevertheless it was kept within the nobility. To return to the importance of military prowess: though in the 18th century knights were no longer so bold, a military career was still held in high esteem and the descendants of the feudal barons were called the *noblesse d'épée.*

The second tradition that played into the evaluation of men in the 18th century consisted of certain other deeply-rooted elements of the Christian system of values and beliefs. It was in the Christian tradition above all that universalistic values had been kept alive throughout the Middle Ages, when otherwise particular relations between men had the strongest moral enforcement. Though the Church went along with the lay definition of the social hierarchy and divided men into God's priests, fighters, and workers, ultimately all these were *equal* before God—they were brothers in God. All men were equally sinful, and they were equally able to attain grace and salvation; Christian teachings even gave the weak and humble a definite advantage over the proud and powerful where the attainment of salvation was concerned. In any case, saintliness was not the prerogative of kings or nobles. Anyone familiar with medieval church architecture will remember that the contributions of humble artisan groups to the building of a cathedral were as welcome and as significant as those of the nobility. The Church visible and invisible belonged to all alike. Furthermore, the Church always provided an area in which a certain freedom of opportunity existed—the regular and secular clergy was open to anyone with a calling, and the humblest man could become part of the prestigious priestly order. While it is hard to estimate precisely the vitality of

Christian universalism in the 18th century, it provided a certain basis for secular universalism to build on when the pressures for the recognition of ability and competence increased.

Third and finally, we come to the contribution made to the 18th century system of stratification by what might be called "modern" developments. These developments are modern only in the sense that they persist today and that from our point of view they are still the latest development. The tradition referred to is that which recognizes successful performance in socially important roles of any kind, and which approves of social mobility as the result of such success. These attitudes toward achievement arose chiefly in connection with the activities of men of business, though, as we have seen, they were also current to some extent in the military world. Success in the growing business world, whether in commerce, finance, or industry, was largely the result of personal competence, and the success was so striking, and so important in terms of the total economy, that occupational roles in this area won prestige and recognition in spite of traditional contempt for them. The businessman, like the early knight, was a mere "self-made man"; nevertheless, his property was such as to command respect regardless of his ignoble heredity. It was through the rise of the world of business especially that the approval of mobility—limited approval to be sure—was introduced into the stratification system of 18th century France.

*mobility*

It is necessary to discuss somewhat further the interplay of these historical traditions and the mixture of types of stratification systems that they produced in 18th century France, in order to create a better picture of how men were socially evaluated at that time:

1. *Elements of Caste.* At birth, as we have seen, every individual was either a nobleman or a *roturier*, and performed either the prestigious functions which were associated with the nobility, or those functions which were traditionally defined as worthy of less respect. The noble class preempted

political and high religious authority, it owned a considerable amount of land, and the careers of military officer and diplomat were chiefly noble. The non-noble class performed commercial, professional, and laboring roles. The rigidity with which these functions were hereditarily segregated varied in the course of the century. Noblemen could engage in commerce only to a very limited extent and still maintain their nobility. As for the *roturier*, his limited access to traditionally noble roles was increasingly restricted, and by 1781 a *roturier* was legally prohibited from obtaining a commission in the army, and informally he was completely excluded from high ecclesiastical offices. Another caste feature of the society was the relatively unchangeable status accorded to the nobleman, depending on the degree of nobility of his family and, above all, the closeness of its blood relationship to the royal house. Also, the age of the nobility of a family determined its status for all time. Even in the *roturier* class, many bourgeois pointed with pride to the fact that their families had been bourgeois rather than workers or peasants for many generations.

2. *Open Class Elements.* We have seen to what extent the disapproval of mobility tended to fix the class lines of the society and made for the hereditary segregation of social functions. However, France in the 18th century was a society in which there was also limited approval of social mobility, and this gave it some characteristics of open class. The channels of social mobility took two forms: one gave legal recognition of the achievement of important social roles by the conferral of nobility, the other gave only informal but often equally cogent recognition. Certain kinds of political authority, which could be bought, conferred legal nobility, as did also personal recognition by the king of major services (most generally money) rendered to the monarchy. The attainment of great wealth could lead to informal equality with the nobility, symbolized by intermarriage and intimate social relations. Furthermore, occupational success within the *roturier* roles

made it possible to "marry up" within the hierarchy of that class. To give only one example, the son of a petty merchant, who *rose* to be a lawyer, could marry a lawyer's daughter.

The wealthy *roturier* could not only acquire some of the functions of the nobleman and some of the concomitant prestige, he could also attain a close approximation of the noble way of life. By the 18th century, many *roturiers* owned homes like those of the nobility, dressed like the nobility, imitated their recreational activities, and, like the noblemen, felt it beneath their dignity to work for a living. The significant thing to note here is that this noble way of life *could* be followed by some men of *roturier* origin with relative impunity, though not without some moral conflict.

3. *Primary and Secondary Patterns.* The moral conflict we speak of above was the consequence of the coexistence in French society of two sets of institutions with contradictory normative, or moral, prescriptions. The more strongly institutionalized of the two patterns was that of approval of the existing class hierarchy and disapproval of mobility; thus French society stood somewhat nearer the pole of caste than that of open class. This primary pattern was institutionalized throughout the whole population of the society, *roturier* as well as noble, but in the actual system of concrete social interaction a secondary pattern of mobility had developed increasing importance. With this increasing importance, the secondary structural pattern also became institutionalized to a limited degree. A delicate and ultimately fragile adaptive mechanism, the acceptance, more specifically the *ennoblement*, of the mobile *roturier*, preserved the integration of the system. But for the *roturier* especially, the contradictory norms approving and disapproving mobility created strain and conflict. The destruction in the later 18th century "feudal reaction" of the adaptive mechanism, of the possibility of ennoblement which had been available to the *roturier* for several hundred years, may have made the bourgeoisie more sympathetic to the revolution of 1789.

It was the bourgeois groups in particular—the highest segment of the larger *roturier* group—that was oriented toward and availed itself of the opportunities for mobility in the Old Regime. By and large, the bourgeoisie accepted the status hierarchy with which it was confronted, and sought to improve its position by means of the approved channels of mobility. But the strong emphasis the bourgeoisie placed on the secondary patterns came to endanger the very existence of the primary ones. The nobility, which had a strong vested interest in the caste elements of the society, attempted to eliminate the open class patterns, and thereby greatly intensified the bourgeois conflict of values. It is this ambiguous situation in which the bourgeoisie found itself, and its ambivalent feelings toward that predicament, which constitute the main focus of interest of this study, because in this situation may be found some of the seeds of the bourgeoisie's endorsement of the Revolution of 1789.

For while the present investigation does not attempt to deal with the actions and attitudes of the bourgeoisie after the outbreak of the French Revolution, the theme of "Equality" is far too prominent both in the ideology and the social actions of the revolutionaries not to cast a shadow backward in time over the problem of the social mobility of the 18th century bourgeoisie. To be sure, on the subject of the French Revolution there has been too much reasoning backwards from consequences to causes. However, since one very important aspect of the French Revolution was a change in the class structure of France, a change in the criteria for evaluating the individual and in the attitudes toward social mobility, it seems useful to attempt to relate an analysis of the earlier class structure to this climactic change.

After the French Revolution, those secondary patterns of stratification which had been institutionalized only to a limited degree, and especially among the French bourgeoisie of the 18th century, became the patterns of predominant importance. And it was the bourgeoisie which under the slogan of "Liberty, *equality*, fraternity!" led the Revolution and profited most greatly from it. While in the *ancien régime* the nobility had been the strategic class in the society—strategic in the sense that its values were representative for the society as a whole—it was the bourgeoisie that took over that strategic position after the Revolution. An analysis of the position of the bourgeoisie in the class structure of 18th century France will, we hope, help to explain the role the bourgeoisie played in changing the class structure of French society.

# CHAPTER II

## The Composition of the Bourgeois Class and Its Internal Differentiation

IN legal terms, 18th century French society was divided into only two social classes, the noble and the non-noble (or *roturier*) class. These two legal classes corresponded also to broad social definitions of class status. The legal definition of classes was derived from the traditional hereditary segregation of social functions in feudal society, in which the land-holding military aristocracy was rigidly separated from the peasantry and the small artisan class. The superior class of nobles had from the beginning considerable internal differences of wealth and authority, but its social functions remained limited, down to the 18th century, to the holding of political authority, including diplomatic service, to military careers and high ecclesiastical offices. The inferior peasant and artisan classes, however, became increasingly differentiated, not only in terms of property, but also in function. Out of these classes grew both the bourgeoisie and the industrial working class, all performing traditionally non-noble functions down to the 18th century.

Within both these so-called social classes, then, we find a large number of sub-classes, groups of families with the same style of life, who intermarried and treated each other in other respects as equals. Within the nobility, important determinants of a family's position were the age of its lineage, the extent of its political authority in feudal terms (i.e., duchies, counties, etc.), its relation by blood to the royal house, and its current wealth and political authority. The exigencies of court etiquette made it necessary to set up a fairly precise hierarchy of statuses within the nobility;[1] the internal structure of the *roturier* class was less clearly defined.

---

[1] H. Brocher, *Le rang et l'etiquette sous l'ancien régime* (Le Mans, 1936), *passim*.

Our chief problem here is, first, to delimit that section of the *roturier* class that we may legitimately call the bourgeoisie, and, second, to attempt to establish the internal differentiation of this bourgeois class. There is no consensus, however, either among men of the 18th century or among later historians, as to the precise limits of this class. The two main criteria used by both are, first, occupation and other aspects of the style of life, and second, the amount of property, but vast discrepancies in these two respects between individuals cause some confusion. There were even, as we shall see, great differences in the "other aspects of the style of life" between individuals with the same occupation.

In defining the lower limit of the bourgeoisie, one 18th century observer, Yves Besnard, for example, would allow bourgeois status only to the *rentier*, who lived off his income, and not to anyone actively working.[2] Other contemporaries, though, did not define the occupational possibilities compatible with bourgeois status so narrowly. For the lawyer Barbier, one of our most useful informants on 18th century society, his hard-working colleagues at the bar were unquestionably good bourgeois. Very few contemporaries would have questioned the bourgeois status of financiers, industrialists, and wholesale merchants, but the status of the shopkeeper was less clear. The shopkeeper's way of life, if not his actual work, was similar to that of the artisan who did manual labor, and *it was manual labor that was most generally considered as incompatible with bourgeois status*. The greatest ambition of the 18th century ancestors of Paul Déroulède, for instance, was to leave behind them their trade of tailoring. By the middle of the 18th century, these Déroulède were proudly established in the lower ranks of the legal profession.[3]

Later historians have tried as best they could to reflect contemporary opinion in deciding what occupations to use for

[2] F. Y. Besnard, *Souvenirs d'un nonagénaire* (Paris, 1880), I, p. 143.
[3] Leopold Olivier, "Les Déroulède sous l'ancien régime. Essai de réconstitution d'un livre de raison," *Souvenirs et mémoires*, IV (1900), p. 129.

their definition of the bourgeoisie. Since the class lines at the lower end of the hierarchy were blurred in actual social inter-action, and the historian cannot even use the traditional social-legal line that existed at the upper end, for practical purposes he must be somewhat arbitrary. Aynard, in his analysis of the French bourgeoisie, draws the line only against manual labor,[4] and we accept this decision, while acknowledging its arbitrariness. Fage, for example, in his history of the 17th and 18th century Tulle, excludes small merchants and shop-keepers from the bourgeoisie, "for we speak here only of those inhabitants *vivant bourgeoisement*."[5] He thinks that the bourgeois were those owning real estate, engaged in com-merce and the liberal professions, as well as those having ca-reers in the official financial administration—treasurers of France, controllers of the king's domain, *receveurs de taille*, etc.

If we draw the lower line at manual labor, we draw the up-per limit short of the *noblesse de robe*. In spite of the social-legal line separating the noble and *roturier* classes, there is some confusion, both among contemporaries and later his-torians, about the relation of the *noblesse de robe* to the bour-geoisie. This group was ennobled not for feudal military service, but for political and, chiefly, legal service to the monarchy in more recent centuries. The *robe* was drawn from the bourgeoisie, and since, until the 18th century at least, they lacked the prestige of the *noblesse d'epeé*, some his-torians like Lacroix and Aynard, and even Bouchard in his excellent history of Dijon, consider the *robe* as only the high-est group in the bourgeoisie.[6] Contemporaries, too, tended to lump all ranks of the legal profession under some such head

[4] Joseph Aynard, *La bourgeoisie française: essai de psychologie* (Paris, 1934), p. 240.

[5] René Fage, *La vie à Tulle aux 17e et 18e siècle* (Paris, 1902), p. 28.

[6] Paul Lacroix, *Le 18e siècle, institutions, usages et coutumes. France 1700-1789* (Paris, 1875), p. 69; Aynard, *La bourgeoisie française*, pp. 313-314; Marcel Bouchard, *L'évolution des esprits dans la bourgeoisie bour-guignonne* (Paris, 1929).

as "le Palais" or simply as "the bar," with the noble magistracy at the top. With some degree of arbitrariness, again, and for some reasons which will become evident in our later discussion of mobility patterns, we prefer to consider the *robe* definitely as part of the nobility.

Apart from determining the lower and upper limits of the class, another problem in delimiting the composition of the bourgeoisie is presented by the clergy. Confusion with respect to the clergy arises from the fact that in legal terms the clergy formed a separate and privileged estate, the old "First Estate." For the purpose of class analysis, however, the clergy must be divided in the way it was divided in actual social relations—into the upper clergy and the lower clergy. The upper clergy was drawn almost entirely from the nobility, the lower from the *roturier* class, and there was almost no mobility from the lower into the upper clergy. The lower clergy should here be included in the bourgeoisie, since, on the whole, it was the professional bourgeoisie which constituted most nearly its social equals.

Finally, another group that it is difficult to place unequivocally either in the noble or non-noble class are the intellectuals. The problem here is quite different from either the case of the *robe* or the clergy. The root of the difficulty is the fact that in the group of leading writers and thinkers of the 18th century, the traditionally approved hereditary segregation of occupational functions between nobles and *roturiers* breaks down. Although men of *roturier* origin did predominate in this group, there were also many noble intellectuals. Sedaine and Rousseau, for example, came from the laboring class, Duclos from the bourgeoisie, while Montesquieu and d'Holbach were nobles. Furthermore, though these men shared the function of intellectual activity, their styles of life differed as widely as their class origins. Many of the intellectuals made a living from other occupations than that of writing, and these occupations ranged from the large-scale business activities of Voltaire and Beaumarchais to the rather pitiful music-copying of Rousseau or to the political sinecures of Duclos and Marmontel. Some were able, more and less successfully, to live from their writings: Sedaine did fairly well as a popular if not brilliant playwright; Diderot did less well from the income of his philosophical writings.

For all these reasons the position of the intellectuals with relation to the bourgeoisie in the 18th century is not clear-cut, though it is fairly clear that the function of the intellectual was traditionally *not* a noble one. Although medieval scholastics and Renaissance humanists, men like Aquinas and Erasmus, had enjoyed high regard, the function of the intellectual had never been explicitly dignified by nobility, and survivals of the old definition of this profession as non-noble can be seen in the 18th century. Sénac de Meilhan felt that literary renown was not unaccompanied by ridicule for a nobleman, and that "learning and intellectual perception were in some sense *roturier* qualities; in ranging himself among writers, a man of rank seemed to lower himself into an inferior class."[7] Montesquieu's literary success made him ineligible for a diplomatic career, and such men as Bernis, Turgot, and Choiseul did what they could to conceal their intellectual activities.[8] These activities were not *dérogeant*, as was commerce, but they were not quite honorable either. We shall try, presently, to establish the position of the intelligentsia within the bourgeoisie.

If we draw the lower limit of the bourgeoisie short of manual labor, and the upper limit short of any kind of nobility, whether of the sword or the *robe*, we may include the following two large groups of social functions in the bourgeois range: first, the world of business, that is, industry, commerce, and finance, and, second, the professions, under which heading would come law and medicine, and to a lim-

---

[7] G. Sénac de Meilhan, *Du gouvernement, des moeurs et des conditions en France avant la révolution, avec les caractères des principaux personnages du règne de Louis XVI* (Hamburg, 1795), pp. 181-182.

[8] Henri Carré, *La noblesse et l'opinion publique au 18e siècle* (Paris, 1920), p. 208.

ited degree the lower clergy and the intellectuals. Our next step must be to determine the internal hierarchical differentiation of the bourgeois class, to find the sub-classes within the bourgeoisie, in order to prepare the way for our later discussion of ways of life and of mobility patterns.

In establishing such a bourgeois hierarchy, it is first of all necessary to make a distinction between local and national scales of ranking. Only rarely did "big fish" from provincial towns receive equally respectful recognition in Paris, which would have been for them the symbol of national importance; the fame of the great bourgeois of Paris was more likely to reach the provinces of France. Secondly, in local ranking, it is necessary to bear in mind the predominant occupational orientation of the population of a given town, whether it was a seaport, or a provincial capital, or an industrial center. The difference between local and national prestige is fairly obvious and requires no illustration, but a few examples will show how prestige hierarchies varied according to the types of towns involved. The two Breton towns of Rennes and Nantes illustrate this variation nicely. Rennes was the provincial capital and seat of the Parlement of Brittany, and the *gens de loi* were without doubt the most important people in town. The merchants of Rennes were not only economically dependent on the parlementary population and on all the litigants the courts brought to Rennes, but also they esteemed the legal profession as superior to their own occupation.[9] In Nantes, however, as also in Saint-Malo or Brest, the shipowners and *négociants* were undisputedly the leaders in all municipal affairs.[10] When we come to Bordeaux, one of the

[9] Armand Rébillon, "Recherches sur les anciennes corporations ouvrières et marchandes de la ville de Rennes," *Annales de Bretagne*, XVIII (1902), p. 14; Henri Sée, *La vie économique des classes sociales en France au 18e siècle* (Paris, 1924), p. 184 ff. Sée indicated that the prestige difference existed in spite of the fact that many lawyers were *capités* lower than the *gens de finance* and merchants.

[10] Sée, *Classes sociales*, pp. 145-146; Maurice Bernard, *La municipalité de Brest de 1750 à 1790* (Paris, 1915), p. 23; also, Henri Sée, "Le rôle de la bourgeoisie bretonne à la veille de la Révolution," *Annales de Bretagne*, XXXIV (1919-1920), p. 406.

greatest seaports of France, we find the wealthiest shipowner-merchants figures of not only local but national stature.

Given these limitations set by the local character of any particular bourgeois hierarchy, it is nevertheless possible to abstract from the many scattered pieces of evidence about intimate social behavior, about respect or deference, a composite bourgeois hierarchy, and before we proceed to a discussion of it, it seems desirable to make a diagram:

| *Business* | *Professions* |
|---|---|
| financiers and *négociants* | intellectuals |
| industrialists and merchant-manufacturers | lawyers |
| | doctors |
| wholesale merchants | lower clergy |
| retail merchants, shopkeepers | law clerks, assistants[11] |

We have then, in effect *two parallel* hierarchies within the bourgeoisie, with a certain rough correspondence between the levels of the two, and we shall sketch them in turn, bringing out the correspondence where we can.

1. *The Professions.* The elite of the professional group was formed by the intellectuals, who, by and large, were evaluated in terms of their social functions *qua* intellectuals,

[11] It is worth comparing this hierarchy with one set up in Poitiers, which divided society for the purpose of marriages and funerals according to the *droit curial* and *salaire du sacristain* paid:

1. magistrates, nobles or those living nobly, lawyers, doctors, wholesale merchants, directors and receivers of the tax farms. *Droit curial*, 8 livres.
2. notaries, solicitors, merchants and others, living from a non-manual occupation. 6 livres.
3. artisans, having a mastership in a manual occupation. 4 livres.
4. all other inhabitants, like store clerks, journeymen, domestic servants. 3 livres.
 (See Marquis de Roux, *La Révolution à Poitiers et dans la Vienne* [*Mémoires de la Société des antiquaires de l'ouest*, 3e série, IV (1910)], pp. 30-31.)

This hierarchy corresponds to our own in two important details: in the significant dividing lines formed, first, by manual labor and, second, by the distinction between the wholesale merchant and the shopkeeper.

rather than on the basis of their varying class origin. Their especially high prestige in the 18th century seems to be directly related to the enhanced importance of their function. In the moral confusions and contradictions of that century, when the basic values of the aristocratic society were being called into question, the function of the intellectual of clarifying, expressing, and developing the fundamental values of the society became more urgently important. Of all the bourgeois, only the intellectuals and the wealthiest financiers had very close social relations with the nobility.

Next in importance among the professions was that group of occupations composed of the lawyers, doctors, and lower clergy. It was a legal career, especially, that the small shopkeeper hoped his son would achieve, and everywhere, in Paris as well as the provinces, the pull was away from trade towards this profession and toward minor public offices.[12] All except the wealthiest businessmen were considered to have an inferior status by the professional bourgeoisie, and therefore the best talents in business families were drawn into the government or the liberal professions.[13] The legal profession gained prestige from its close association with the *robe* at the Palais, and with the dignified ceremonial of court procedure.[14] The law was apparently attractive although it was well known that it was an overcrowded profession and not a remunerative one. Lawyers could be found anywhere from the 16th to the 20th class of the 22 income classes set up for the payment of capitation in 1696, and therefore paid from 30 livres down to as little as 3 livres.[15] Still, of the nine sons of Jean-Baptiste Accarias, a merchant of Grenoble, two became lawyers, four

---

[12] Albert Babeau, *Les bourgeois d'autrefois* (Paris, 1886), p. 136; Fage, *La vie à Tulle*, p. 81.

[13] David Landes, "French Entrepreneurship and Industrial Growth in the 19th Century," *Journal of Economic History*, IX (May, 1949), p. 56.

[14] Fage, *La vie à Tulle*, p. 82.

[15] Baron Francis Delbèke, *L'action politique et sociale des avocats au 18e siècle. Leur part dans la préparation de la Révolution française* (Louvain, 1927), p. 131.

went into the Church, and two chose military careers.[16] The future *constituant* Mounier, also of Grenoble, went into the law, and this was considered the normal thing for the son of a "marchand aisé" to do.[17] (More will be said below about the *dérogeant* nature of commerce.)

The fact that a legal career was rewarding in terms of prestige rather than of wealth is brought out again and again. Barbier, who often spoke of the self-respect bordering on pride and vanity of the lawyers (meaning, barristers), also revealed that in a certain conflict, the lawyers simply could not afford to go on strike against the Parlement; for some of them it would have meant a drastic reduction in their standard of living, for others it was a question of their very subsistence.[18] Berryer remarked on the large number of lawyers at the Paris bar the year he was admitted, many of whom, he thought, had chosen their career for its prestige alone.[19] Even by the middle of the 17th century, the *avocats* were no longer able to compete with the wealthy businessmen for offices in the high *robe*. (Of this we shall say more later.) Also, in the later 17th century and in the 18th century a serious legal abuse aversely affected the income of the barristers, and, to some extent, their relative prestige. For instead of insisting on the oral pleading of cases, as was required by law, the judges of the Palais accepted written briefs, a practice which was as much to the disadvantage of the *avocats*, or barristers, as it

[16] Joseph Accarias, "Un publiciste dauphinois au 18e siècle: Jacques Accarias de Sérionne, sa famille, sa vie, et son ouvrage," *Bulletin de l'académie delphinale*, 4e série, III (1889), p. 499.

[17] F. Vermale, "Les années de jeunesse de Mounier (1758-1787)," *Annales historiques de la Révolution françaises*, XVI (1939), p. 5.

[18] See E. J. F. Barbier, *Journal historique et anecdotique du règne de Louis XV*, publié pour la Société de l'histoire de France d'après le manuscrit inédit de la Bibliothèque Royale, par A. de Villegille (Paris, 1847-56), II, p. 120; the author used also a later edition of Barbier's diary, *Chronique de la régence et du règne de Louis XV, 1718-1763* (Paris, 1857-75), and the two editions will henceforth be referred to as *Journal* and *Chronique* respectively.

[19] Berryer, *Souvenir de M. Berryer, doyen des avocats de Paris, de 1774 à 1838* (Paris, 1839), I, p. 49.

was to the advantage of the *procureurs*, or solicitors.[20] In spite of such setbacks, however, the position of the *avocats* was, on the whole, an enviable one, and it does not appear to be merely a lag from an earlier period when their power was greater.

The social contacts of the 18th century lawyers reveal the respect in which they were held. Society sought them and they liked to be sought, and they brought their solid knowledge and sensible concern for public welfare into the salons.[21] The lawyer Mathieu Marais had social contacts with high *robe* families like the Nicolai or d'Aguesseau, Barbier knew d'Argenson personally, and Moreau as a young lawyer "had dinner in the best company."[22] These lawyers we have mentioned were very deferential to their *robe* friends, but a few like Gerbier lived like grand seigneurs and consorted with the nobles as equals. Gerbier often visited the salon of Mme. Geoffrin, and another well-known lawyer, Target, went to the salon of the Maréchal de Beauvau. The more eminent lawyers were very likely benefiting from that same need for social enlightenment felt by the educated laity which enhanced the social status of the intellectuals in the years before the Revolution. Boulloche is probably only slightly carried away by enthusiasm for the subject of his biography, Target, when he concludes that "a new life is beginning for the Bar, and, on the eve of the Revolution, the legal profession is already considered to be one of the finest and most enviable of all . . . next to that of the intellectuals."[23]

Doctors, like lawyers, seem to have been considerably respected in the 18th century. The very fact that long years of study were necessary to become a doctor insured that the doctors came from well-to-do bourgeois families with private incomes, and once established they lived well, if not in great

[20] Louis Ducros, *La société française au 18e siècle, d'après les mémoires et les correspondances du temps* (Paris, 1922), p. 145.

[21] P. Boulloche, *Un avocat au 18e siècle: Target* (Paris, 1893), p. 31.

[22] Delbèke, *Les avocats au 18e siècle*, p. 119ff.

[23] Boulloche, *Target*, p. 31.

style. They intermarried with good legal families or high commercial ones.[24] The surgeons had always been ranked well below the doctors, until the 18th century, on account of the traditional combination of surgery with the trade of the barber. But by 1747, Barbier reported strong professional rivalry between doctors and surgeons, and he attributed this to the threatened superiority of the doctors. Increased skill on the part of the surgical profession and the high favor of M. La Peyronne, the first surgeon, with the king, had greatly enhanced the position of surgeons in the public's eyes.[25] Through royal favor, a royal declaration was issued separating the surgeons from the barbers, with whom they had been ignominiously associated for over a hundred years, and requiring a certificate of study of all surgeons.[26]

Although the priesthood must in some sense be considered an occupation of a different order of dignity from that of law or medicine, dealing as it does with sacred subjects, the career of the cleric can be seen to be a profession similar to that of the doctor or lawyer. This equivalence is substantiated by such evidence as that presented by Roux, that in 18th century Poitiers the law and the Church were considered to be roughly equal career possibilities from the point of view of the bourgeois: " 'The two main careers open to the bourgeoisie were the Church and the Palais,' said the *conventionnel* Thibaudeau, and his father, one of whose brothers had been the priest of Sanxay, chose them for his sons: 'My brother, who had natural wit, was dissipated, did not like to study, fell behind in his work. Without consulting us, it was decided to make him a priest and me a lawyer.' "[27] Since, furthermore, diocesan law in the Poitiers region demanded that the *curé* have a private income of at least 80 livres, the peasantry was excluded from ecclesiastical careers and for the bourgeois it

[24] Babeau, *Les bourgeois*, p. 107ff.
[25] Barbier, *Journal*, ii, pp. 365-366.
[26] *Ibid.*, p. 366.
[27] Roux, *La Révolution à Poitiers*, pp. 23-24.

presented about the same expense as one of the lower judicial offices. "[The] merchant or master artisan who had saved [this amount] spent it with equal pride to clothe his son with either [clerical or legal] robes."[28] In some parts of France, however, in Anjou, for example, a career in the lower clergy ranked somewhat below the law.

2. *Business.* So much for the hierarchy within the professions. Let us turn next to the business complex of occupations, where we shall discuss the shopkeeper, the wholesale merchant and industrialist, and finally the overseas *négociant* and financier, in order of increasing importance. The sentiment concerning the lesser dignity of the *boutiquier*, the retailer as compared to the wholesaler, was indeed strong, and we find this distinction, sometimes phrased as that between the *marchand* and the *négociant*, made repeatedly. Jacques Savary, author of the *Parfait Négociant*, writing in the late 17th century, shared the popular prejudice of *magasin* against *boutique*.[29] Another nice example of the distinction can be found in the reply of the Chamber of Commerce of La Rochelle to a query by the local intendant as to whether a certain man was to be considered a *marchand* or a *négociant*: "The rank of *négociant* is generally given to anyone engaged in commerce; however it applies more particularly to the wholesale merchant, who sells in a warehouse in large lots. The merchant is the retailer who holds an open shop and sells any amount or weight. . . . *Négociants* are found only in commercial centers of a certain size, and the market towns or smaller towns have only merchants."[30] In his discussion of 18th century Tulle, Fage thinks that the shopkeepers hardly keep up a bourgeois style of life,[31] and the same thing is true, of

[28] *Ibid.*, pp. 24-25.
[29] Henri Hauser, "Le 'Parfait Négociant' de Jacques Savary," *Revue d'histoire économique et sociale*, XIII (1925), p. 11.
[30] Emile Garnault, *Le commerce Rochelais au 18e siècle* (Vol. I, *La réprésentation commerciale de La Rochelle*), (La Rochelle, 1888), p. 97.
[31] Fage, *Vie à Tulle*, p. 28.

course, of the lowest ranks of the professional bourgeoisie, the tipstaffs and bailiffs connected with the courts.[32]

Large-scale industrialists of the modern type were very few in 18th century France. Far more common was the "marchand ayant manufacture," the large-scale merchant who ran a small industry on the side, so that the two groups of industrialists and wholesale merchants overlap to some extent. The double role of the merchant-manufacturer gave him considerable local if not national importance. In Montpellier, for instance, the "négociants ayant manufacture" ranked in importance second only to the greatest shipowner-merchants in town.[33] The same was true in Nantes.[34] There were some industrial families of importance in pre-revolutionary days: the de Wendels, who started their first factory at Hayange in Lorraine in 1704;[35] the Dolfus' textile fortune was growing in the area around Mulhouse and the Oberkampf's at Jouy; and the Ferrey family dominated the silk industry at Lyon.[36] Except for the de Wendel family, however, these families were only locally respected. The Van Robais were the most important citizens of Abbeville, and lived in the isolated grandeur of seigneurs.[37] At Nevers, too, the pottery manufacturers were the most influential citizens of the town, and the wealthiest among them, Jérome Lestang, had a fortune of 500,000 livres. At least five other merchant-manufacturers followed behind him with 200,000 livres, each,[38] and such wealth put them far ahead of almost all bourgeois except the millionaire financiers.

[32] *Ibid.*, p. 84.

[33] Louis J. Thomas, *Montpellier, ville marchande* (Montpellier, 1936), p. 183.

[34] Sée, "Le rôle de la bourgeoisie," p. 406.

[35] Louis Launay, *De Wendel* (Vaucresson, 1938), p. 7.

[36] Pierre Gaxotte, *Louis XV and his Times*, J. L. May transl. (Philadelphia, 1934), p. 306.

[37] Georges Ruhlmann, *Les corporations, les manufactures et le travail libre à Abbeville au 18e siècle*, Préface d'Emile Coornaert (Paris, 1948), pp. 73-74.

[38] Louis Guéneau, *Les conditions de la vie à Nevers à la fin de l'ancien régime* (Paris, 1919), pp. 596-597.

Some of these successful industrialists did become socially intimate with members of the nobility. This was especially true of bourgeois entrepreneurs in the mining industry, for, in spite of the problem of *dérogeance*, this was an area of industrial activity in which there was considerable noble participation. This shared activity enhanced the prestige of the bourgeois industrialists and led to a rapprochement between bourgeois and noble in their social as well as their business lives and created a relatively unified group of entrepreneurs; in part, this was accomplished by the assimilation of the bourgeois participants to the noble way of life.[39] An example of this kind of success is also the English industrialist, John Holker, who developed textile mills in Normandy and was highly respected both in Rouen and Paris: "He had become one of the most remarkable representatives of that new working aristocracy, and the aristocracy of birth, which was increasingly participating in large industrial enterprises, recognized its merit, though it also on occasion forgot its social menace. . . ."[40]

The wholesale merchant was in general a respected member of the business bourgeoisie, whether or not he carried on industrial enterprises, and the elite of this group ranked with the financiers in importance. Fage remarks that commercial success stood behind almost all *haute bourgeois* families in Tulle.[41] At Rouen, commerce is said to have been the most important occupation, and it constituted the most common subject of conversation.[42] The town of Valenciennes had a commercial elite, "composed . . . of the merchants selling cambric, lawn and batiste, among whom were the families of Fizeaux, Hamoir, Cannonne, Desvignes and Mestives."[43] Hamoir *père*

[39] Marcel Rouff, *Les mines de charbon au 18e siècle, 1744-1791* (Paris, 1922), pp. 238-241.

[40] André Rémond, *John Holker, manufacturier et grand fonctionnaire en France au 18e siècle, 1719-1786* (Paris, 1946), p. 118.

[41] Fage, *La vie à Tulle*, p. 80.

[42] Grace Gill-Mark, *Une femme de lettres au 18e siècle. Anne-Marie Du Boccage* (Paris, 1927), p. 10.

[43] Adrien Legros, "Les dépenses d'un bourgeois de Valenciennes à la veille de la Révolution," *Revue du Nord*, VIII (1922), p. 210.

left to *each* of his eight children 98,000 livres.[44] Next to the great pottery merchants, who formed the elite in Nevers, ranked the merchants of the town;[45] and at Rennes, they ranked next to the lawyers.[46]

When we come to seaborne commerce, we find a group of merchants who had no equals within the business complex of the bourgeoisie other than the financiers. The renown of these great *négociants* was less than that of the financiers only because their notoriety was less. The wealthiest merchants of Bordeaux or Marseilles were highly respected locally as well as in the capital, and men like Gradis, Bonnaffé, or Bethman in Bordeaux shared local social honors with the nobility.[47] Proof of Gradis' social arrival was his large share of stock in the *Grand Théâtre* of Bordeaux, for all the stockholders were friends of the Duc de Richelieu, governor of Guyenne.[48] These *négociants* of the coastal towns had, in fact, something the financiers always lacked: real roots in the social and political life of their native cities.

Unlike most other French businessmen of the time, except perhaps the financiers, the *négociants* and *armateurs* were men of enormous resources and willing to take risks, large risks, in their enterprises. Their fortunes and their fleets were immense. Marseilles had generally profited greatly from colonial trade and reflected the wealth of the colonies, and "the Roux brothers were as wealthy as they could wish to be. Their fortune was said to be 30 million livres. . . ."[49] François Bonnaffé of Bordeaux ended with a fortune of 14 million francs and a fleet of 30 ships, and Gradis and Journus gave

---

[44] *Ibid.*, p. 211.

[45] Guéneau, *La vie à Nevers*, p. 597.

[46] Rébillon, "Les corporations de Rennes," p. 17.

[47] Richard Brace, *Bordeaux and the Gironde, 1789-1791* (Ithaca, 1947), p. 9; Jean de Maupassant, "Un grand armateur de Bordeaux. Abraham Gradis (1699?-1780)," *Revue historique de Bordeaux*, VII (1914), pp. 334-335.

[48] Maupassant, "Abraham Gradis," p. 334.

[49] Adrien Artaud, "Georges Roux. Etudes historiques sur le 18e siècle," *Revue de Marseilles*, XXXII (1886), p. 326.

their transatlantic enterprises an unparalleled scope and vigor.[50] Although Gradis' parents were rather impecunious Portuguese merchants, he himself was "'the famous Jew, Gradis! . . . one of the kings of Bordeaux,'" and at Paris he was received as an equal by *fermiers généraux* and by courtiers.[51] The leading *négociants* of Montpellier, like François Durand, had important commercial empires, though they ranked below those of Bordeaux or Marseilles.[52]

These men engaged in overseas commerce, together with the financiers, constituted a social world which, while it was bourgeois, was really quite apart from the rest of the bourgeoisie. Though fundamentally they shared the same occupational function, the scale of their operations and the splendor of their way of life was so different as to constitute almost a difference in kind. This was particularly true of the financial group within the bourgeoisie, who abandoned the traditional bourgeois way of life to a greater extent than the *négociants*, and it is with a discussion of the financiers that we end our sketch of the bourgeois hierarchy. While merchants, doctors, and lawyers treated each other more or less as equals, financiers (and *gros négociants*) were not even remotely of their kind, and they treated them with a kind of hostile respect, a grudging fascination. There is little indication that the lower bourgeois felt any class loyalty towards the financial elite, or had any pride in its achievements, prestige, and power. As we have already suggested, the great *fermiers généraux* of Paris did not have even the local geographical ties which made the populations of Bordeaux or Saint-Malo wish to honor their great *armateurs* with high municipal offices.

The power and influence of the financiers—farmers general and royal bankers—was indeed very great in this period when the French treasury relied on these private manipulators of

[50] Alfred Leroux, *Etude critique sur le 18e siècle à Bordeaux* (Bordeaux, 1921), pp. 176-177.

[51] Maupassant, "Abraham Gradis," p. 288.

[52] Thomas, *Montpellier*, p. 185ff.

wealth for its income. They had public functions without public responsibilities, and though the very great private profits they made as royal tax collectors were legitimate, their lack of responsibility nevertheless aroused much hostility as well as fear. Indicative of these attitudes towards the financiers is that same flavor of exaggeration we find in writings about them that is current today in some discussions of the influence of Wall Street. In Darigrand's *Anti-financier*, for instance, there is the familiar picture of the financier who is the ultimate manipulator of all power and who uses it solely to his own advantage and to the detriment of society: "Is it possible that all these ills brought on by the scourge of Finance do not open people's eyes? Is it possible that people watch calmly while the greatest houses are supported by the gold of the Financiers, while the only rich houses are those of the Financiers, or of financial origin . . . while the principal groups in the Nation are united in their complaint against Finances and no one wishes to trace to its origin that immense wealth which makes so many people grumble against that iniquitous profession, Finance?" And his answer is that *no one* can afford to attack the financiers, because finance controls everything, "and to crown the evil, ennobles all."[53] Thirion's later estimate of them is similar and has to our ears the ring of vulgar Marxism, when he claims that these men not only controlled the national purse-strings directly, but also influenced the monarch by mistresses out of their ranks, the nobility by family ties, and the intellectuals by their subsidies.[54] Along with the popular belief in the omnipotence of the financiers went the conviction that they were essentially dishonest or crooked. Barbier spoke for many when, again and again, he referred to the financiers as *fripons* or scoundrels. John Law was a *fripon*,[55]

---

[53] Jean Baptiste Darigrand, *L'Anti-financier, ou Relève de quelques unes des malversations dont se rendent journellement coupables les Fermiers-Généraux*, . . . (Amsterdam, 1763), pp. 69-70.

[54] Henri Thirion, *La vie privée des financiers au 18e siècle* (Paris, 1895), p. 32.

[55] Barbier, *Chronique*, I, pp. 63-64.

Samuel Bernard was a great scoundrel,[56] and when the Pâris brothers were exiled during the Regency period, he spoke of them, in turn, as "great scoundrels, but extremely clever. . . ."[57]

Partly as a result of this exaggerated and hostile view of the integrity of the financiers, though also, of course, on account of their scandalously large profits, the financiers were on several occasions made the scapegoats and their fortunes were confiscated when the royal treasury was all but bankrupt. The enormous credit they extended to the government could be very lucrative, but it might also result in collapse if the government withdrew its protection and in the so-called public interest declared its debts null and void. In 1715, and again after 1760, the plight of royal finances made a further increase in the national debt a less attractive policy than a reform of the tax farming system, and the efficacy of these popular measures and the real precariousness in the status of many of the financiers are shown by the waves of bankruptcies in these periods. In spite of *real* reforms under Louis XVI, when the Revolution came the financiers were still so closely associated with the hated social and political institutions of the Old Regime that several of them, most notably Lavoisier, went to the guillotine. It is possible to speculate along several lines about the origins of this popular hostility. Popular hostility had, undoubtedly, tangible social sources in the ill-concealed corruption and fraud which were associated with high finance in general, and practiced by the tax farmers in particular. But, also, we might ask, was this hostility the reaction of people who resented the achievement of so high a status in a society that disapproved of mobility? Or does it, perhaps, represent the sublimation of hostility toward this very fixity of status and the displacement of aggression from the nobility to a safer object, the financial elite? Neither hypothesis can be tested, and both have a certain plausibility in the light of our analysis of the value conflicts inherent in French class structure.

[56] *Ibid.*, pp. 89-90.    [57] *Ibid.*, p. 44.

The foregoing account of the popular distrust of and hostility toward the financiers should not, however, lead to the
inference that finance did not enjoy very high prestige in the
social hierarchy. Resentment was always mixed more or less
heavily with respect and admiration, less so among the people
and the conservative old bourgeoisie, more so in noble and
intellectual circles. Among the intellectuals, quite a change in
attitude toward the financiers is evident between La Bruyère,
writing at the end of the 17th century, and Duclos in the
middle of the 18th. For La Bruyère, finance was a filthy occupation, corrupting the soul, while Duclos condemned only the
excessive ostentation of the suddenly rich but did not assume
that the process of making money itself was necessarily despicable.[58] Finance even came to compete as a desirable career
with the *robe*, and both Duclos and Barbier note and deplore
the growing preference among the very wealthy for financial
rather than parlementary offices: "Before the Regency, [ac-
cording to Duclos] the ambition of the farmer general was
to make his son a parlementary counselor. . . . We have just
seen an ecclesiastical counselor, who was even a sub-deacon,
quit his office in order to go into finance. I do not doubt that
there may not at all times have been magistrates sufficiently
despicable to be so greedy, but they would not have dared
to do so openly."[59] Barbier reported, for example, that the
*fermier général*, M. de la Reynière, who married his daughter
to M. de Malesherbes of the old *robe*, wanted nothing more
from the king than that he grant the survivance of the office
of *fermier général* to his son. The nobility by birth, which, as
we shall see in greater detail later, was intermarrying a great
deal with this bourgeois elite, necessarily had at least to moderate its disdainful attitude toward its new relatives, and to

[58] M. Roustan, *Les philosophes et la société française au 18e siècle* (Lyon, 1906), pp. 195-196.

[59] Charles P. Duclos, *Considération sur les moeurs de ce siècle* (Londres, 1784), pp. 291-292.

some extent respectful relations developed between the two classes.

We now have a fairly complete sketch of the internal differentiation of the bourgeois class. An appreciation of the existence of two parallel hierarchies within the bourgeoisie— one professional and the other business—and especially an intimation of the large range of statuses within these two hierarchies will prove very helpful when we come to discuss the problems and conflicts inherent in bourgeois class status.[60] Different groups within the bourgeoisie had very different reactions and attitudes toward the class system and toward their own position in it, and this brief "Who's Who" of the bourgeoisie is important to the understanding of conflicts of values, attitudes toward mobility, problems related to the appropriate style of life, and finally of accepted mobility patterns.

[60] For another sketch of the composition of the bourgeoisie, which breaks that class down somewhat differently, see Philippe Sagnac, *La formation de la société française moderne* (Paris, 1946), II, pp. 57-70.

# CHAPTER III

# Fundamental Values — Religious and Secular

IN every human society answers must be provided to problems of other than empirical reference, problems beyond the scope of science and common sense. These problems are inherent in the conditions of man's life, and it is man's fate to have an emotional and intellectual appreciation of them. Man must give meaning and purpose to life and death, to good and evil, to justice, and to such human experiences as good and bad "luck." It is the function of religion to provide the basic definitions of "the nature and destiny of man" and of the "good life" that will lead to the fulfilment of this destiny. Ultimately, in almost all religions, this destiny is achieved in a life-after-death, by rebirth in a world substantially and, by and large, physically different from the one in which man now finds himself. In this scheme of things, the life "here and now," in human society, may be given a greater or lesser degree of importance, and may be evaluated as more or less worthwhile. And man himself may be defined as a helpless and insignificant tool of the Divine, or as a relatively responsible and dignified actor.

Since the vast majority of men in society cannot dedicate their lives exclusively to the achievement of perfection in religious terms, for a society of saints could not function adequately, the religious attitude toward life in this world is of great importance. There may be more or less strain between the good religious life and the life of social usefulness, between the achievement of salvation and the successful performance of social obligations. In the Christian religion, the dualism between the spirit and the body and the definition of man's life on earth as relatively worthless have always caused considerable strain for the good Christian, and the compromises of the Church-in-the-World have been among the chief foci of tension in Western history.

1. *Catholic View of Man and Society.* The traditional Catholic religion condemned sinful man to a life of toil and misery in this world, but held out the hope that by the subordination and conquest of his "lower" nature, of his this-worldly desires and ambitions, he might attain eternal happiness after death. Man's interest in his activities in his life on earth must always be subordinated to his supreme interest in salvation, and the Church taught man how best to adapt his life in the world to the demands of religious morality. In the process of this adaptation, lay institutions were brought as far as possible under the Christian banner: the feudal knight was transformed where possible into a crusader, and the supreme feudal political authority, the king, was made directly responsible to God by his consecration with holy oil. At the time of the greatest moral authority of the Christian religion in the High Middle Ages, even economic institutions, which naturally had the greatest potential this-worldly orientation, were regulated in such a way as to minimize the advantage accruing to the individual merchant or artisan. The strict controls of the guild organization, and especially the prohibition of usury, limited wealth in consonance with the good Christian life.

The medieval Christian was dependent on the Church for the attainment of his salvation. He could not be saved without the mediation of the priesthood, and he had to accept without doubt or explanation the Church's teachings about the proper conduct of life. Fundamental truth was believed to have been revealed for all time by God, and the scope of rationality was limited to efforts to explain the physical world in the light of revealed truth. Once this revealed truth had been brought into rational accord with nature and society by the great theologians of the Christian Church, there was a strong bias in favor of considering not only the original truth but also the subsequent rationalizations as permanently valid. If existing theology could be tampered with at all, it had to be changed by men in high ecclesiastical authority, never by laymen. The Church did not tolerate lay scholasticism any more than lay claims to new revealed truth. It must be noted, however, that it was *critical* rationalism rather than reason and logical procedure that were suspect.

Catholic teachings concerning the life in society of Christian man assumed that man was by nature disposed to do evil, and it was to avoid this sinful disposition that the Church preached the necessity of submission to the established religious and secular authorities. Catholic teachings could not be questioned, even when they concerned empirical problems; in fact, the areas of empirical and non-empirical problems were not strictly separated. Christians were taught that the secular authorities and, indeed, the secular class structure were divinely approved as well as hallowed by human tradition. God had created priests, fighters, and workers and though ultimately they were equal in the sight of God, during their temporal existence priests and fighters had a traditional superiority that could not be infringed.

2. *Secular Morality*. By the 18th century, however, there was a large segment of the French population which found the Catholic definition of the good Christian life inadequate, and the concentration on salvation prescribed by Catholic doctrine too restricting. The economic activities of the new-born 12th and 13th century bourgeoisie could, without excessive strain, be regulated in conformity with the traditional other-worldly orientation and authoritarian conservatism. As social values in other areas of life became more and more secular, as politics, art, and learning, for example, became secularized, and as, furthermore, the commercial and industrial bourgeoisie became an ever larger minority of the population, so it became more difficult for this bourgeois class not to assert, to some extent, the this-worldly and rational assumptions underlying its work and its life. A more general secular morality

was now conceivable, and for the bourgeoisie, which had no place in the traditional religious and aristocratic conception of man and society, it provided a meaningful definition of its human condition.

Among the aristocracy, too, this secular morality flourished in the 18th century; indeed, nobles of a somewhat intellectual bent were among the first to abandon traditional religion for deism and even atheism. However, the alienation of these nobles from the traditional view of man's nature and destiny arose in philosophical and ideological sources, rather than in their customary activities, as was the case with the bourgeoisie. Many of the nobles were intense and articulate in the expression of their secular beliefs, but it may be doubted whether these beliefs formed an integral part of their lives to the same extent that they did in the lives of the bourgeois, even though the latter group might be far less intense and articulate. But in such matters we can only speculate.

The new secular ethic oriented man to the possible goods of this world, be they conceived in terms of the full realization of his potential abilities in work well done, of respect and esteem by his fellowmen for his achievements, or of wealth and the pleasures and comforts of the flesh. This new definition of the virtuous life has often been called the "lay morality." Lay morality is a very broad concept, and it includes a number of different things. The bases of all its aspects were a this-worldly orientation and a shift of responsibility for the attainment of virtue from the Church to the individual. The individual must strive for a good life within man's allotted life span, and it is up to him to find the right ways and means. This-worldly happiness becomes a matter for rational pursuit. Utilitarian considerations might prescribe the short-run postponement of pleasure and happiness, but these were not entirely postponed beyond the limits of life on earth. At the beginning of the 18th century, lay morality was primarily concerned with bringing more enjoyment into the lives of individuals,[1] but as the century progressed, such men as Diderot, Toussaint, LaMettrie, and Duclos, to name only a few, shifted the emphasis from personal happiness to more humanitarian concerns. Morality became the science of social as well as personal welfare, and personal conduct had to be justified in terms of social good.[2] It was assumed that a morality of this kind had application to all mankind, and Caraccioli wrote in his *Réligion de l'honnête homme*, "that independently of any religion, nature inspires man with a certain love of Justice, which is sufficient to make an upright man [*honnête homme*]."[3]

Barbeu du Bourg, in his *Petit Code de la Raison Humaine*, held three things necessary *and sufficient* for bourgeois happiness: good health, good sense, and a good conscience; and these were accessible to any *honnête homme*. This *honnête homme* was no longer so pessimistic about his own nature, in the tradition of the Christian pessimists, who denied to sinful man the possibility of, or the right to any happiness in this life. André Morize has gone so far as to say that in one part of the bourgeoisie it was felt that "beside the sin of greed and sensuality there was room for the sin of abstinence."[4] The man of the middle bourgeoisie, at least, was a moderate man in all his activities and ideas. M. Grosley, for example, recounted the following criteria for respect and esteem in his middle-class home: ". . . one must know how to live frugally and have no debts; one must do no harm of any kind to anyone; nor do harm to oneself, either by neglecting one's affairs and letting them fall apart, or by any excess ruinous to

[1] Daniel Mornet, *Les origines intellectuelles de la Révolution française (1715-1787)* (Paris, 1933), pp. 41-42.

[2] *Ibid.*, pp. 110, 43-44.

[3] Quoted in Bernhard Groethuysen, *Origines de l'esprit bourgeois en France* (Paris, 1927), p. 291.

[4] André Morize, *L'apologie du luxe au 18e siècle et "Le Mondain" de Voltaire* (Paris, 1909), p. 28. See also M. Gaffiot, "La théorie du luxe dans l'oeuvre de Voltaire," *Revue d'histoire économique et sociale*, XIV (1926), pp. 320-343.

health.""⁵ Those who lived up to these maxims died peacefully; those who did not died as badly as they had lived.⁶ It is significant that in this moral life neglect of the affairs of this world was as much frowned on as excessive indulgence of the flesh.

This new secular this-worldly orientation gave the bourgeois the possibility to find meaning and dignity in his activities. For the bourgeois had no noble conception of his role defined by the Church as did the aristocracy, "for his part, he would never know any grandeur but the artificial one, based only on human industry and ambition."⁷ The bourgeois was a self-made man, and he claimed recognition for his achievements in defiance of the Church and of tradition. In doing so, the bourgeois assumed a much greater share of the responsibility for his salvation than the Catholic Christian was supposed to. Instead of depending only on God-given order and justice in the world, the bourgeois took upon himself the responsibility for the planning of his life, and for the consequences of his planning. Through rational calculation and hard work he tried to control his environment and gain the security he formerly depended only on God to grant.⁸

3. *Compartmentalization of Values.* The *honnête bourgeois* did not, of course, discard his interest in salvation or neglect his observance of religious ceremonies. He tended not to mix religion and business. In the area of his life which had especially great emotional significance, namely his family life, and in crises where he was confronted with unusual danger and uncertainty, the bourgeois turned to religion for meaning and security. Regular Sunday churchgoing by the whole family was definitely still customary in the 18th century. Besnard reported "the heads of families, especially in the bourgeoisie, rarely missed attendance at high mass in the parish, and they

⁵ Grosley, *Vie de M. Grosley* (Londres, 1787), p. 17.
⁶ *Ibid.*, p. 18.
⁷ Groethuysen, *L'esprit bourgeois*, p. 284.
⁸ *Ibid.*, p. 172.

were accompanied by their children."[9] The big events of family life, births, marriages, and death were always accompanied by all the appropriate religious ceremonies and sentiments. The *livres de raison*, in which were recorded the important expenses of family life, and hence indirectly the important events, show that until the middle of the 18th century, at least, all temporal affairs were still placed formally under divine protection.[10]

The need for a sense of divine justice is probably felt most keenly when men are faced with the problem of death. The 18th century bourgeois who felt he had the necessary resources to cope with the problems of day-to-day existence, needed to seek solace in the face of death, his own or that of his loved ones, in the teaching and rites of the Church. In wills and testaments there were large bequests to the Church, and provisions for burial, masses, and annual services.[11] In the presence of death, man bowed to God's judgment and put himself at God's mercy; social and empirical methods of control and calculation were ineffective.

It was the occupational sphere, of course, that was the focal point for the application of secular values by the bourgeoisie. More particularly, in the world of business rather than in the professions, rational calculation without regard for tradition was essential for success, and this success was measured not in terms of religious morality, but by a more quantitative measurement of the value of the enterprise. Business had to be conducted honestly, and the businessman hoped that he was working under God's benevolent protection, but beyond that, *how* he conducted his business did not concern God or the theologians.[12] The world of business had a rationale and an ethic of its own, and empirical critical rationality brought success according to the special criteria established for this sphere of action. For most bourgeois, therefore, the Church's disap-

---

[9] Besnard, *Souvenirs*, I, p. 49.
[10] Babeau, *Les bourgeois*, p. 326.    [11] *Ibid.*, p. 326.
[12] Groethuysen quotes Turgot on this point, *L'esprit bourgeois*, p. 272.

proval of the lending of money at interest was simply unwarranted interference with the necessary and proper methods of conducting business, and the Church's long battle against usury was a failure. The Gradis of Bordeaux, though they were Jews, were no different from their Christian fellow businessmen in their attitude toward God in their business relations: "They were convinced . . . of the validity of the proverb: God helps him who helps himself; and having paid their respects to God, after expressions of mutual regard and wishes for good health, they quickly got down to business."[13]

Just as the traditionalism and authoritarianism of the Church were felt to be obstructions to the successful conduct of business, so also were the traditional particularistic relations among men, which had the Church's support, in contradiction with desirable business methods. Brotherly love and respect for social class differences are irrevelant to the process of buying and selling, and though the 18th century businessman was still far from freeing himself from the traditional restrictions of competition, his success depended to a large extent on such emancipation. The essentially universalist-egalitarian spirit of commerce was, indeed, recognized by contemporaries. Séras, for example, realized, that if the nobleman was ever to become an effective merchant, he would have to learn to treat other merchants as equals in his business relationships, and never "pull his rank."[14] Superiority of birth was irrelevant to the functionally specific relations of commercial activity. J. J. Garnier realized, furthermore, that this universalism in commerce was a threat to traditional political institutions when commerce became sufficiently important to affect "the spirit of the nation"; he felt that when the spirit of the nation *was* the spirit of commerce, this led inevitably to the downfall of the nobility.[15] One had only to look at England and Holland.

---

[13] Maupassant, "Abraham Gradis," p. 186.
[14] P. Séras, *Le commerce ennobli* (Bruxelles, 1756), pp. 26-27.
[15] Jean Jacques Garnier, *Le commerce remis à sa place. . . .* (?, 1756), p. 28.

The successful businessman had to defy the Church's disapproval of the conduct of business on a competitive basis; he
had to break with the traditional values that proscribed individual initiative and destroyed individual incentives. Henri
Sée thinks that the Jews, who had never shared fully in the
values of the Old Regime, and the Protestants, who had broken
with the Church and had been rejected by the Old Regime,
were on the whole more successful in trade than the Catholics,
because they felt no obligation to abide by the traditional rules
of the commercial game, which forbade independent action
and competition.[16] The new type of industry inevitably came
into conflict with the old guild organization through which
the medieval-Catholic conception of economic relations was,
in part, enforced. New and secret technical inventions constituted one important focus of conflict; such individual ex-
ploitation of knowledge and skill violated the old guild
rules.[17]

The old *special* rights and privileges which protected men
against competition did not suit many of the rising bourgeois,
who were eager to risk their financial resources in the ex-
ploitation of new mechanical inventions. "Industries left towns
where the regulations were still in force, and established themselves in the country."[18] Barbier reported, in passing, a suit
between the powerful Six Corporations of Paris and the great
manufacturer Van Robais, which may be considered to be a
symptom of the conflict.[19] However, it does not do to exag-
gerate the extent to which the French businessman of the
18th century had become emancipated from the traditional,
particularistic conception of economic relations. The Van Robais, themselves, for instance, were still almost as much privi-
lege-oriented as were the corporations: "they had the same

[16] Henri Sée, "Dans quelle mésure puritains et juifs ont ils contribué au
progrès du capitalisme moderne?" *Revue Historique*, CLV (1927), pp. 57-68.
[17] Rémond, *John Holker*, p. 22.
[18] Charles Morazé, *La France bourgeoise, 18e-20e siècle* (Paris, 1946),
pp. 70-71.
[19] Barbier, *Chronique*, I, p. 64.

concern to guard their monopoly jealously and even to extend their privileges as much as possible."[20] It was very difficult for French entrepreneurs to make the necessary break with the traditional web of particularistic privileges that circumscribed the merchant in the corporation.

Since we have suggested a definite religious influence on the traditional economic organization, it is relevant at this point to raise the problem of the influence of Jansenism on the values of the French bourgeoisie. The controversy about Jansenism continued in France through the first half of the 18th century, and a large part of the Paris bourgeoisie was Jansenist, according to Barbier. Jansenism and Calvinism have considerable superficial similarities, and since Calvinism has been shown to have had some definite connection with the rise of the capitalist middle class, it might be supposed that Jansenist beliefs would play a similar role in shaping the development of French capitalism. Calvinist asceticism, for example, played an important part in the accumulation of wealth on the part of the Calvinist businessman, and the Jansenists, by all accounts, led sternly ascetic lives. But on closer analysis it would appear that Jansenist asceticism did not have that same quality of "this-worldliness" that Weber perceived as so important a component of Calvinism.[21]

Basic both to early Calvinism and to Jansenism were the beliefs in the predestination of salvation and in the individual and irresistible experience of grace. Both doctrines had a very lofty conception of the power of God and a great pessimism about the nature of man. Such a God as theirs could not be influenced by man's actions, however meritorious they might seem. However, predestinarianism when carried as far as it was in this early Calvinist and Jansenist theology creates serious ethical and psychological problems, for man in society can hardly be exempted from all responsibility for his actions,

[20] Ruhlmann, *Abbeville*, p. 76.
[21] Max Weber, *The Protestant Ethic and the Spirit of Capitalism*, T. Parsons, transl. (London, 1930).

nor can most men face throughout their lives the possibility of eternal damnation.

While these acute strains are inherent in both Calvinism and Jansenism, they were resolved somewhat differently in the two cases. In later Calvinist preaching, the assumption was made that *all* men were called. Furthermore, the Calvinists came to introduce the concept of a covenant between God and man, a covenant which, in effect, bound God to the salvation of virtuous men.[22] Virtuous men worked purposefully and hard to establish God's greater glory in the world—and to promote the welfare of their commonwealth. The Jansenist, however, never departed from the strict interpretation of predestination. Only the few received God's grace and only they were to be saved. But all Jansenists alike sought to conduct their lives as nearly as possible in accordance with the will of God. Every one of their daily actions was a moral one, and it might or might not be a useful, or rational, one.[23] The Jansenists' purpose in life was not to work actively for the greater glory of God on earth, but the more passive, traditional Lutheran-like purpose of fulfilling the mission to which God had designated them. The whole Jansenist orientation was deeply conservative.[24]

These different adaptations to the problems of predestinarianism are, at best, only partly responsible for the emergence of the active, successful Calvinist capitalist, on the one hand, and the passive, tradition-bound Jansenist bourgeois, on the other. The whole social and economic context in which the two systems of belief developed was, of necessity, in interaction with these beliefs. The Jansenists were influenced not

[22] For a discussion of the covenant concept, see Leonard J. Trinterude, "The Origins of Puritanism," *Church History*, xx (March, 1951), and Sidney A. Burrell, *Kirk, Crown and Covenant*, unpublished Ph.D. dissertation, Columbia University, 1953.

[23] Groethuysen, *Buergerliche Welt- und Lebensanschauung*, ii, pp. 43-44.

[24] Paul Honigsheim, *Staats und Soziallehren der Franzoesischen Jansenisten im 17ten Jahrhundert* (Heidelberg, 1914), p. 151 ff., especially, and *passim*.

only by the doctrinal conception of their relation to the Catholic Church, but by the fact that they were identified, broadly speaking, with French Catholicism as against secularism.[25] And Jansenist economic traditionalism must be considered in relation to the general economic "backwardness" of France, both in industry and agriculture.

Although the conservative Jansenist, then, did not have great success in the tradition-breaking business field, willy-nilly he was forced into political opposition by the condemnation of his beliefs as heretical. As Jansenism became a political issue, by the support of the monarchy of papal condemnation, the conservative opposition of the Parlements to the monarchy became identified with Jansenism, and many a Jansenist lawyer found himself, almost reluctantly, to be a political free-thinker. In the 18th century, the Jansenists formed, if not a radical, at least a combative, "frondeur" segment of the population. The lawyer Target came from such a Jansenist legal family: "one of those bourgeois parlementary families, so numerous in France, for which the Jansenist maxims imposed on religion an ascetic complexion, and for which submission to the monarchy was no longer possible without a certain quarrelsome independence; one of those families, in fact, wonderfully prepared . . . to receive the teachings of the thinkers and the *philosophes*."[26] Paradoxically, perhaps, their very conservatism forced many Jansenists to adopt a generally anti-authoritarian attitude, in opposition to both the Church and the monarchy, but they were far from being secular rationalists.

More or less, then, the bourgeois of the 18th century had carved out for themselves a sphere of activities in which a secular morality was operative, in which the values that guided their conduct were distinct from the traditional religious and social values. Businessmen, especially, but lawyers also, had managed to compartmentalize their values, restricting the

[25] Groethuysen, *Buergerliche Welt- und Lebensanschauung*, II, pp. 69-70.
[26] Boulloche, *Target*, pp. 8-9.

"new" secular ones to the occupational sphere of their activities, and keeping their private and family life in the framework of the old religious definition of the meaning of life and death. We say "more or less," because within the bourgeoisie there were great variations in the delimitation of the value compartments, and in the success with which they maintained any such separate compartments. These variations ranged from the complete abandonment of religion by the atheists to almost unconscious admission of some of the secular values by devoutly religious men. Most bourgeois, excepting the intellectuals, were not, of course, aware of this coexistence of religious and secular values in their *Weltanschauung*; they had, at best, a very crude explicit formulation of their own values. Where these values *were* made explicit, the conflict between religion and secularism often became focused on the issue of the acceptance or rejection of the ideas of the *philosophes*. The *philosophes* and their writings became for many relatively unsophisticated bourgeois the symbols of secularized thought; the rationalism of the *philosophes* was more dramatic evidence of the growth of secularism than the critical rationalism the bourgeois applied unawares in his business and professional activities.

It is possible for us to illustrate the spectrum of bourgeois reactions to the new secular values, but unfortunately it is not possible to do any better than guess at the number of bourgeois who adopted the various attitudes. Our guess would be that, until the middle of the century at least, the majority of bourgeois accepted without very much strain the segregation of their values into two compartments, but that the claims of religion were still strong, and that too frank a declaration of secularism caused considerable discomfort. At the religious end of the spectrum, the teachings of the *philosophes* were rejected out of hand. In the journals of the royal historian Narbonne, or of the lawyers Siméon-Prosper Hardy and J. N. Moreau, the enlightenment is clearly condemned as immoral; (even in the manner of condemnation though, times had changed since the Middle Ages: the enlightenment is no longer described as the work of the devil).[27] M. Tamisier, a "bon bourgeois" of Marseilles, was not even aware of the threats to established beliefs. "[He] had remained entirely ignorant of the religious controversies"; and he died without doubts about his salvation.[28] Hardy, in remarking on the great number of suicides that occurred in Paris, deplored the decline of morality as the cause of these occurrences. He attributed "conduct so much opposed to Christianity and to religion" to the "complete decline of those teachings drawn from sound and pure morality, whose preachers and supporters have been persecuted for so long."[29] He revealed here his own piety and the threats that he saw in those times to such piety. Another example of a strongly religious man was the merchant Etienne Desloges of Caen, who, as a zealous Catholic, was scandalized at the creation of a Masonic lodge in the city in 1742.[30] And though the father of Bergasse, the *constituant* lawyer, was a merchant and four of his five sons went into trade, his son reported that he was given a strictly religious upbringing at home.[31]

Times were changing, however, and many bourgeois either took an explicit interest in new ideas or adhered to them without awareness that they were doing so. Bouchard says of the 18th century bourgeoisie at Dijon that it now "had the courage to reason without prop or guide."[32] In the Academy at Dijon men toyed with Rousseauistic ideas about a golden age in the state of nature, or about the union of virtue and hap-

[27] Mornet, *Les origines intellectuelles*, p. 213.

[28] Octave Teissier, *La maison d'un bourgeois au 18e siècle* (Paris, 1886), p. 40.

[29] Siméon-Prosper Hardy, *Mes loisirs; journal d'évènements tels qu'ils parviennent à ma connaissance (1764-1789)*, publié d'après le manuscrit autograph et inédit par M. Tourneux et M. Vitrac (Paris, 1912), p. 323.

[30] G. Vanel, *Une grande ville au 17e et 18e siècle. La vie publique à Caen. Moeurs et coûtumes* (Caen, 1910), p. xxv ff.

[31] *Un defenseur des principes traditionnels sous la Révolution. Nicolas Bergasse. Avocat au Parlement de Paris. . . . * Etienne Lamy, ed. (Paris, 1910), pp. 3-4.

[32] Bouchard, *La bourgeoisie bourguignonne*, p. 587.

piness—in all innocence and without hostility to existing institutions: but these men would one day understand Rousseau
in all his revolutionary implications.[33] This new courage to
reason describes the situation well, for many bourgeois, even
those who continued to be religious, felt they had a kind of
choice in this matter. They did not take religion for granted;
"philosophy" had come into existence and it had to receive
consideration.

Even a pious lawyer like Mathieu Marais, who shunned
any of the more advanced salons and did not care for either
the young Voltaire or for Montesquieu, and who still claimed
to believe in miracles, read with enormous curiosity much that
was destructive of tradition. His special hero was Bayle, and
he tolerated such intelligent skeptics as St. Evremond in spite
of their libertine morals.[34] Barbier, too, was no radical, or
even "liberal" in the modern sense, but for the very sake of
his "bourgeois peace"[35] he limited his religious zeal and recommended such limitation to other bourgeois. He felt, for example, that no respected member of the Parlement should be
involved too deeply in religious disputation, either for or
against the Catholic Church, and he condemned a M. de
Montgéron "who for the sake of the so-called truth sacrifices
his worldly goods, his status and his freedom . . . ";[36] such a
one could only become a bad example. Likewise, he felt that
"bourgeoisie oblige" the first president of the *Cour des Aides*
not to go to see a woman in convulsions of a supposedly mi-
raculous character.[37] Barbier disapproved of the condemnation
of the *Encyclopédie* by the censors, for this would only arouse
the curiosity of the simple faithful about matters that did not
concern them.[38] This is an interesting point, for, while Barbier

---

[33] *Ibid.*, p. 612 ff.
[34] Mornet, *Les origines intellectuelles*, p. 64; Mathieu Marais, *Journal et mémoires sur la régence et le règne de Louis XV (1715-1737)* (Paris, 1863-1868), *passim*.
[35] Mornet, *Les origines intellectuelles*, p. 65.
[36] Barbier, *Journal*, II, p. 164.
[37] *Ibid.*, II, pp. 4-5.
[38] *Ibid.*, III, p. 339.

felt that this literature was potentially disruptive of the morality of the *peuple*, he himself felt no apparent qualms about
reading not only the banned *Encyclopédie*, but also Toussaint's *Moeurs*, of which he procured a copy after considerable
trouble.[39] In 1759 he also read Helvetius' *De L'Esprit*, which
was definitely atheistic in nature. While not as cynical as Voltaire, who is said to have remarked that if God did not exist,
it would be necessary to invent Him for the masses, Barbier
shared Voltaire's aristocratic prejudices that the enlightened
critical rationalism was only for the educated elite. Barbier
was still a religious man, but one who rejected the authority
of the Church in many areas where it irked him—in those
areas he felt it was controlled by bigoted Jesuits.[40]

Many bourgeois who did not investigate the new ideas of
the *philosophes* and who continued to attend Church were
nevertheless no longer "bourgeois catholiques," but rather
"bourgeois et catholiques."[41] In his biography, the later *conventionnel* Thibaudeau made some revealing comments about
his parents, especially his father, in this connection: "My
mother, an excellent woman, devoutly religious and devoted
to her household, took care of our education, both physical
and religious. My father did not concern himself with it, ab-
sorbed as he was with the work in his occupation. As lawyer
to the bishop of several chapters and convents, he went to
Church but he was an admirer of the *philosophes* and a deist.
Morning and evening, he said his prayers, his hat in hand,
walking, according to the season, in his garden or in his study.
Sundays and holy days, our mother took us to Church."[42]
Thibaudeau's mother could be described as still a Catholic
bourgeoise, while his father was perhaps somewhat religious
and mostly bourgeois.

As for Thibaudeau himself, he represents the secular ex-

---

[39] *Ibid.*, III, pp. 34-35.
[40] Barbier, *Chronique*, II, p. 26.
[41] Groethuysen, *L'esprit bourgeois*, p. 35.
[42] A. C. Thibaudeau, *Biographie. Mémoires 1765-1792* (Paris, Niort,
1875), pp. 52-53.

treme of the spectrum, in spite of all his mother's efforts to give him a religious education. Without even very much soul-searching, or intellectual effort, Thibaudeau turned against his religious upbringing. The frequent and obvious sinfulness of so-called Christian man no longer inspired him with fears of hell, but served only to discredit religion in his eyes:[43] "As a child, I had faith and religious fervor; but as the result of being threatened with hell, I had more fear of the Devil than love of God. As an adolescent, I loved religious cere-monies as spectacles; I sang hymns and psalms in the choir. As a young man, I went to Church only out of fear of social disapproval, and for altogether secular purposes, in spite of good examples shown to me by my family. The world of-fered me bad ones too. I saw libertines and disreputable peo-ple pretending devotion, priests of dubious morality. . . ."[44]

The progress toward atheism of the little bourgeoise Ma-non Phlipon, better known as Mme. Roland, shows the path that someone of more intellectual bent than Thibaudeau took. Mme. Roland started life as a conventionally brought-up Catholic girl, whose mother, she said, was pious and devout, and conformed to the broad principles of the Church's teach-ing, if not to the details.[45] Manon recalled in her *Memoirs* that she was full of awareness of the importance of her first communion,[46] and she spent several happy years being edu-cated in a convent school. Even then, perhaps, there was a

---

[43] In both the case of Thibaudeau and of Mme. Roland, whom we shall discuss below, it must be remembered, though, that their memoirs were written when the revolutionary shift in social values was an accomplished fact, and when it was virtuous and desirable rather than risky to have had skeptical or athetistic views in earlier days. This does not mean that Mme. Roland and Thibaudeau did not actually have moral and intellectual ex-periences such as they describe; it is merely a caution to the reader to re-member that some degree of hindsight may have affected the writers' mem-ory.

[44] Thibaudeau, *Biographie*, p. 53.

[45] Marie Jeanne Roland de la Platière, *Oeuvres de J. M. Ph. Roland, femme de l'ex-ministre de l'intérieur* (Vol. I, *Mémoirs*) (Paris, 1800), p. 21.

[46] *Ibid.*, p. 21.

"protestant" quality to her religion: "The piety of my young heart found no agreement with jesuitical affectations; this piety was too sincere to be allied with the mockery of bigotry."[47]

Manon, however, was an intellectually curious girl and read a great deal. Her progress, in the course of her literary adventures, from piety to deism is best described in her own words: "The works of theological disputation of Bossuet presented a new pasture to me; favorable as they were to the cause which they were intended to defend, they also brought acquaintance with some of the objections to it, and set me on the path toward reasoning about my faith. That was the first step; it was a long way to the final step of skepticism, at which I finally arrived several years later, after having been, successively, a jansenist, a cartesian, a stoic, and a deist."[48]

Mme. Roland's early doubts were also aroused by the Catholic doctrine of *Extra ecclesiam nulla salus*. Her wide knowledge of different historical epochs and different civilizations made her find "the idea of a Creator, who would consign to eternal torment these innumerable individuals, narrow, ridiculous and atrocious."[49] From doubting this particular article of faith, she found it easy to move on to an examination of all others, and after such initial doubt, she thought, any Catholic must be lost to the Church.[50] Not all Catholics, as we have seen, were as consequential as Manon; hers is a fine example of the road to skepticism and intellectual revolt against authority and tradition, travelled by an alert and lively woman.

In the fashionable world of the salons and among the intellectuals of the period, "incredulité" and skepticism were largely taken for granted, and deism vied only with complete atheism for acceptance. Skepticism in the salons came partly out of serious intellectual malaise and social demoralization, partly also out of a fashionable desire to *épater le bourgeois*. Among the intellectuals, it was critical rationalism and em-

[47] *Ibid.*, p. 50.  [48] *Ibid.*, pp. 50-51.
[49] *Ibid.*, p. 65.  [50] *Ibid.*, pp. 65-66.

piricism that undermined first the conservative, intolerant authoritarianism of the Church, and eventually the authority of God himself. God was at first denied only the ability to intervene in the world of natural phenomena; ultimately, however, 18th century materialists denied the existence of anything but this natural world and limited man's experience to his sense perceptions. God and salvation had no place in this limited universe, and moral responsibility (the materialistic determinist's Waterloo) was defined in terms of concern for social welfare. It is not surprising, however, when we recall the specially religious significance of death, that we find a good number of 18th century deists and skeptics, most notably Voltaire, who received extreme unction on their deathbeds.

Of the general weakening of the moral force of traditional religion there can, thus, be no doubt. The majority of men, though, as Roustan puts it, followed the philosophical avantgarde at a comfortable distance.[51] Most bourgeois were probably more anti-clerical than anti-religious; they believed as a matter of tradition rather than of deep conviction;[52] and they hoped for no helpful intervention from God in their everyday lives.[53] This shallowness of conviction might go as far as the skeptical tolerance and the rejection of any fanaticism by the humanistically inclined Burgundian bourgeoisie[54] which was accompanied by a general receptiveness to, and "lack of strength to resist" new ideas and ideologies.[55] In Hardy's laments, too, we find evidence of the attenuation of faith, which he saw "becoming weaker every day, and on all sides, in a manner which was unfortunately only too apparent."[56]

In making an attempt to estimate the amount of alienation from the traditional values, it is necessary to remember that evidence of alienation is more conspicuous to the historian

---

[51] Roustan, *Les philosophes*, p. 281.
[52] *Ibid.*, p. 250.
[53] Groethuysen, *L'esprit bourgeois*, p. 25.
[54] Bouchard, *La bourgeoisie bourguignonne*, p. 236 ff.
[55] *Ibid.*, p. 588 ff.
[56] Hardy, *Mes loisirs*, p. 377.

than evidence of continued devotion. For alienation is expressed in written records accessible to the historian, while devotion is more generally expressed in actual behavior rather than in writing. And it is likely, though not certain, that the most alienated were also the most articulate. Mornet sums up well the difficulty of calculating with any exactness the number of people who no longer adhered to the old religious values and he makes the following estimate, which is perhaps accurate for all its impressionistic quality: "It is difficult to name the skeptics in the middle and petit bourgeoisie, because no one among them took the trouble, in general, to transmit his name to posterity. We know by chance, thanks to Brissot, that M. Nolleau, the solicitor of Paris, for whom he worked as a clerk, was not a religious man. But there is an abundance of general evidence indicating that if skepticism was far from being predominant, it was nevertheless gaining ground every day."[57]

As skepticism and secularism increased, so also did the strain of conflicting moralities, for only a few bourgeois made a clean break with the traditional Catholic religion. The maintenance of two sets of very different fundamental values in compartmentalized coexistence produced a rather precarious peace of mind, and it was partly because the contradictory implications were not clearly realized that such compartments were possible at all. "It is a primary function of any religion to explain and justify society to the population, and in societies where religious belief is wanting, it falls to popular philosophy to discover some rational order in social relationships and institutions."[58] In 18th century France, the traditional religious justification was competing with "popular philosophy," as far as the bourgeoisie was concerned, and when a greater need for consistent justification was to be felt—as was the case before the century was out—the bourgeoisie might be expected to

[57] Mornet, *Les origines intellectuelles*, p. 139.
[58] W. R. Goldschmidt, "America's Social Classes," *Commentary*, X, no. 175 (August, 1950), p. 175.

formulate it in terms of the popular secular values which were more compatible with its rational interests. Given the conflict of values that was the lot of the 18th century bourgeois, whether he be businessman, educated lawyer, or intellectual, he might be expected to question the traditional definition of social "justice" if it became incompatible with other expectations, when it was no longer unequivocally identified with God's justice.

# CHAPTER IV

# Attitudes towards Mobility, and Their Political Implications

IN the classification and analysis of different types of stratification systems, the attitudes towards social mobility are of strategic importance. Variations between the two poles of open class and caste, as we have already seen, depend to a very large extent on the approval or disapproval by the members of the society of the movement of individuals from one class to another. While in the ideal caste society any such movement is considered to be deviant, in the open class society it has full moral approval. Concomitant with the approval of social mobility is the expectation of its happening. The "justice" or "injustice" that is felt to exist in any given class system will depend on the relationship between the degree of approval of social mobility and the extent to which expectations in that direction are fulfilled. In a hierarchy in which statuses are hereditarily fixed, the execution of one's station in life is sufficient for the preservation of justice and the fulfillment of expectations. In the open class system, on the other hand, the sense of justice will be determined by the extent to which men think they are getting what they "deserve," i.e., by the extent to which their competence is rewarded with upward mobility, regardless of their family connections.

In a society such as that of 18th century France, which stood somewhere between the extremes of the spectrum, there was no complete consistency in the moral attitudes toward mobility, and though disapproval was the stronger of the sentiments, a certain balance had to be maintained if a sense of social justice was not to be destroyed. The maintenance of such a balance was of particular significance to the bourgeoisie, which was the most "mobility conscious" element in the population.

It has been suggested that here, as in other areas of expectation, too great a discrepancy between the expectation of mobility and actual fulfillment results in a state of *anomie*, that is, a partial social disintegration reflecting the weakening of moral norms.[1] The same demoralization will very likely also arise when there is *de facto* mobility without the accompanying moral approval, and it was with discrepancies of both these kinds that the 18th century French bourgeoisie was faced to an increasing extent as the century progressed. Of the impact of these discrepancies we shall say more in a later chapter.

When seen in the most general terms, there appears to be a fundamental conflict in the attitudes of the bourgeois class towards the possibility of mobility in the class hierarchy. For the bourgeoisie approved, on the one hand, of the existing class structure which tended in the direction of a caste system, while, on the other hand, it expected a certain amount of upward mobility, and it aspired, as the *summum bonum*, to the achievement of noble status and to the transmission of nobility to its children. As we have seen in the foregoing chapter, there was a coexistence and potential conflict in bourgeois values between the established values of traditionalism and particularism and those values more compatible with its social and economic interests, universalism and rationalism. In terms of the former set of values, the bourgeois disapproved of social mobility and expected none, and felt uncomfortably guilty about his own and his fellow bourgeois' social ambitions. But in spite of this moral uneasiness, most bourgeois *were* ambitious; they believed implicitly in "just" rewards for wealth and competence and expected to rise in the social scale if they "deserved" to do so, and in this respect their conception of social justice was in accordance with universalist values. For a long time, this very ambivalence mitigated the *anomie* resulting from the discrepancy between expectation of mobility

[1] R. K. Merton, "Social Structure and Anomie," *Social Theory and Social Structure*, pp. 125-149.

and its fulfillment, and it was only when the discrepancy became too great that social guilt about mobility aspirations turned to moral indignation at the frustration of these aspirations.

The majority of 18th century bourgeois did, indeed, hope to work their way up in the social scale, step by step, first within the *roturier* group and ultimately into the nobility. For all their growing secular moral independence, most bourgeois concurred in the traditional social judgment that their occupation and their style of life were inferior to those of the aristocracy, and that even the most successful bourgeois could not compete for social prestige with the nobility. Even the most successful bourgeois—those who had demonstrated their competence as financiers or lawyers, for example—lacked a certain stiffness of self-respect and pride in their achievements. Already at the end of the 17th century, La Bruyère had remarked on the lack of contentment on the part of wealthy men, who could buy so many of the symbols of status, but who had to work so hard for the kind of social status they really wanted.[2] Duclos remarked in his *Considérations sur les Moeurs* that "there are few rich people who at times do not feel humiliated at being considered nothing but wealthy."[3] And the perceptive Mme. d'Epinay described one of the financier's wives as follows: "She was a woman who was somewhat hard and proud, who displayed her wealth, but who nevertheless was inconsolable about being nothing but a financier's wife."[4]

"For centuries the bourgeois, envious of the aristocracy, ... aimed only at thrusting himself into its ranks," says Lefèbvre.[5] To modify a common metaphor, he wanted to have his

[2] J. de La Bruyère, *Les caractères, suivis des caractères de Théophraste*, traduits du grec par le même (Paris, 1824), I, p. 174.

[3] Duclos, *Considérations*, p. 127.

[4] Louise F. P. T. d'Esclavelles d'Epinay, *Mémoires*, Paul Boiteau ed. (Paris, 1904?), p. 7, n. 1.

[5] Georges Lefèbvre, *The Coming of the French Revolution*, R. R. Palmer transl. (Princeton, 1947), pp. 46-47.

cake of bourgeois success and eat it in aristocratic company.[6]
In a revealing novel about the bourgeoisie of Grenoble, Ber-
riat de Saint Prix described the social ambitions of a lawyer's
wife for her son: "Her son would be a Counselor, she would
see him sitting in court, in a red robe, on the *fleur de lys* . . .
she would easily obtain for him a marriage to the daughter
of a family little favored by wealth but illustrious for its
nobility. She would have two grandsons: one would be President in the Parlement, the other, starting as captain in the
cavalry, would easily become a general officer."[7]

Voltaire put the ambitions of the rich man equally neatly
into the mouth of Mathurin in his *Le Droit du Seigneur*: "I
want everything to happen at my pleasure and in accordance
with my wishes, for I am rich. So, father-in-law, listen: To
dignify myself in my marriage, I am turning myself into a
gentleman, and I am buying from the bailliff the flourishing
office of royal receiver in the salt granaries: that's not bad. My
son will be a counselor, and my daughter will raise herself
to some noble family. My grandsons will be presidents: And
the descendants of my lord will one day pay court to mine."[8]
Mathurin clearly accepted the established definition of what

[6] In the next two chapters we shall see how the bourgeoisie executed its
aspirations; at present we are concerned only with expressions of the ambitions themselves.

[7] Jean Egret, *Le Parlement de Dauphiné et les affaires publiques dans la
deuxième moitié du 18e siècle* (Grenoble, Paris, 1942), I, pp. 25-26.

[8] Voltaire, *Le droit du seigneur*, comédie (*Oeuvres de Voltaire*, VI),
(Paris, 1838), scène iv:

> Je veux que tout se passe
> A mon plaisir, suivant mes volontés,
> Car je suis riche. Or, beau-père, écoutez:
> Pour honorer en moi mon mariage,
> Je me décrasse, et j'achète au baillage
> L'emploi brillant de receveur royal
> Dans le grenier à sel: ça n'est pas mal.
> Mon fils sera conseiller, et ma fille
> Relèvera à quelque noble famille.
> Mes petits-fils deviendront présidents:
> De mon seigneur un jour les déscendants
> Feront la cour aux miens.

was prestigious, but he was going to use his wealth to attain what was denied to him by birth, and willy-nilly, he was cast into an ambiguous position toward the very basis of the existing hierarchy.

The hopes for social mobility and even for the attainment of nobility were not restricted to the most successful professional or businessmen bourgeois. Besnard recalled the rather touching and quite unfounded hopes held by two of his old aunts, that one of their kin would become a member of the *robe*: "I do not know where my greataunts learned that the performance of the office of notary by fathers and sons for 200 years would confer nobility. But I often heard them say that their nephew Richard . . . would be ennobled on this basis if he should only live to be fifty years old."[9] Poor Richard never lived to the "required" age, but the story shows how widespread was the hope for association with the *robe*.

Even within the bourgeois class, the same criteria of "ancient" birth and "lineage" were applied, which determined status in the aristocracy: "Bourgeois of old stock were frankly proud of their lineage, careful not to form an improper marriage. Office holding and the professions established among them a hierarchy of which they were exceedingly jealous, and which engendered 'cascades of disdain,' as Cournot put it. Nothing was more pronounced than the ordering of ranks within the bourgeoisie itself. . . . Briefly, the bourgeoisie, looked down upon by the high-born, copied them as best they could."[10]

Duclos was considerably amused at the same phenomenon Lefèbvre describes, the attempts of the bourgeois to show at all costs that their lineage was ancient, even if their "ancestors" were quite disreputable: "I have heard bourgeois of Paris, respected citizens, very loyal to the monarchy, pride themselves on the fact that they were descended from one of the

[9] Besnard, *Souvenirs*, I, pp. 58-59.
[10] Lefèbvre, *Coming of the Revolution*, pp. 46-47.

*Sixteen* of the League, who were hanged."[11] And, finally, it is worth noticing that even the artisan class made similar calculations as did the bourgeois on the subject of the acquisition of higher social status. They planned the rise of their children and grandchildren from artisan, to petit bourgeois (surgeon or solicitor), and thence to doctor, lawyer, or even magistrate.[12]

The low self-esteem of the merchant bourgeois, in particular, and their strong desire to slough off their ignoble occupational status emerge very clearly in some of the discussions of the problem of the *noblesse commerçante.* Commercial activities in any form came close to being the very symbol of a way of life unfitting for nobility, and the *dérogeance* of the nobleman who engaged in trade only added emphasis to the low esteem in which trade was held. The government, which was anxious to take advantage of noble capital for the purpose of promoting French trade, made repeated efforts to exempt wholesale and especially overseas commerce from its traditional stigma by legislation,[13] but all the encouragement the government gave the nobility in this regard had little effect on their participation: "Less than fifty years [after all Colbert's efforts] and after all those edicts and declarations, the only possibility that had been admitted was that of the merchant becoming ennobled, not of the nobleman turning into a merchant."[14]

The publication of the pamphlet on *La Noblesse Commerçante* by the Abbé Coyer, in 1756, aroused a new storm of controversy over the question of *dérogeance.* The concept of a *noblesse commerçante* called into question the traditional

[11] C. P. Duclos, *Mémoires sécrètes sur les règnes de Louis XIV et de Louis XV* (Paris, 1881), p. 17.

[12] Roux, *La Révolution à Poitiers,* pp. 20-21.

[13] Charles A. Foster, *Honoring Commerce and Industry in 18th Century France, a Case Study of Changes in Traditional Social Functions,* Unpublished Ph.D. Thesis (Harvard, 1950), p. 115 ff.

[14] Edgar Dépitre, "Le système et la querelle de la *Noblesse commerçante* (1756-1759)," *Revue d'histoire economique et sociale,* 6e année (1913), p. 145.

hereditary segregation of social function and social privilege,[15'] and, therefore, not only did it appear to threaten the vested rights of the nobility, but also it ran counter to the fundamental class attitudes of the bourgeoisie. The bourgeois class was predominantly oriented towards the eventual acquisition of nobility, and the ennoblement of the successful merchant made far more sense in terms of the social goals of both the nobility and the bourgeoisie than a *noblesse commerçante*.[16] The frequency and cogency with which the counterargument was made—namely, that it would be far better to ennoble the successful merchant than to permit the nobility to go into trade—shows the appreciation by some writers of the nature of the French class structure. The proponents of this point of view all pointed out that such a policy of ennobling the merchant might stop the constant movement of able and successful men out of the merchant class into occupations which *were* compatible with nobility. Already in the late 17th century Savary had deplored this: "In France, as soon as a merchant has acquired great wealth in trade, his children by no means follow him in his occupation but go into public office."[17] This complaint was made also, of course, by Colbert, and it was often repeated in the 18th century. Séras remarked that, while at present every merchant was anxious to acquire a small ennobling office, he might be content to remain a merchant if in this occupation he could hope to attain nobility.[18] France did not have the merchants that England and Holland did, and "One can easily find two reasons for this: one, that *commerce is not held in high esteem here*; the other, that commerce *is not perpetuated in the same families*; the second reason is a consequence of the first. If commerce were to be ennobling, both would cease to be effective."[19] Dudevant, an-

[15] Henri Lévy-Bruhl, "La noblesse de France et le commerce à la fin de l'ancien régime," *Revue d'histoire moderne*, VIII (1933), p. 232.

[16] Foster has a nice discussion of this ambivalence, *Honoring Commerce*, pp. 305-307.

[17] Quoted in Hauser, "Le 'Parfait Négociant,'" p. 12.

[18] Séras, *Le commerce ennobli*, p. 30.      [19] *Ibid.*, p. 35; our italics.

other pamphleteer on this subject, similarly deplored the abandonment of trade by the son of the wealthy merchant, who was so strongly inclined to dissociate himself from the occupation of his father that "he hardly deigned to admit that his wealth was derived from Commerce. . . ."[20] Dudevant devised the neat idea of having commerce become ennobling only in the third generation: "In order that the Frenchman lose his ambition to acquire public office and the weakness of abandoning trade, it would be necessary that commerce itself bring him the nobility he desires, and even that in order to acquire it, he be obliged to remain in commerce."[21] In other words, men like Séras and Dudevant advocated a kind of *noblesse de commerce* analogous to the *noblesse de robe*.

We see, then, that in 18th century France it was the class structure that placed serious obstacles in the way of the full development of capitalism. The fundamental limitations on the dynamism of capitalist bourgeois action came not so much from the fact that the bourgeoisie adhered, predominantly, to the Catholic religion, though this may have had some significance, but rather from the tendency of the bourgeoisie to fly away as quickly as possible from socially despised commerce into occupations that carried greater social prestige. The acceptance of the existing class system by the French bourgeoisie may have been at least as important in stunting the growth of French capitalism as their adherence to Catholicism and the absence of a Protestant ethic to foster the spirit of capitalism. The French merchant seemed to lack any real devotion to his occupation, any sense that what he was doing was satisfying and worth while. The English historian Butterfield has noted the "anxiety" of the French bourgeoisie of the 18th century "to leave the bustle and conflict of economic life at the first opportunity, to be satisfied with a safe but moderate income, to build a fine *hôtel*, to ape the nobility." The bourgeoisie did not reinvest its money in commerce and industry and train

[20] L. H. Dudevant, *L'apologie du commerce* . . . (Genève, 1777), p. 43.
[21] *Ibid.*, p. 49.

its children to carry on the firm. It preferred either to live off its income or to buy offices, or to send its children into the professions, "escaping from the business world which they secretly despised in their hearts."[22] François Durand of Montpellier was a rare merchant, indeed, for when the king sent him the Cordon of St. Michel and letters of nobility for his services in famine relief in 1773, he rejected them, because he did not wish to give up commerce.[23]

The 18th century bourgeois identified strongly with the nobility in his snobbish contempt for everything *roturier*, and especially commercial (though, as we shall see in the next chapter, he had strongly ambivalent feelings about his adopting the noble style of life.) Manon Phlipon, for example, had the greatest contempt for the merchant's goal of making a profit. She declared she "could never lend myself to anything of this kind, nor could I respect anyone who is thus occupied from morning till night."[24] She felt there was no "honnêteté" in the commercial occupation—rather a striking declaration when it is compared to the contemporary English or American identification of virtue and business acumen. She felt that if the merchant was not downright corrupt, he was at least vulgar and uncivilized, and she wrote thus to her friend Sophie of her disdain for the commercial class: "I have no affinity for commerce, my spirit is not suited to it; I fear it for its dangers: I fear it on moral grounds. Besides, (and let this be said without offending those who deserve to be excepted,) there is hardly any education, and even less sensibility, among most people of this class. . . . The desire to amass wealth when they are established, and the difficulty of doing so quickly, gives them a kind of singlemindedness, which, without being obviously deplorable, is nevertheless so to one of sensitive moral sense."[25]

---

[22] H. Butterfield, *The Origins of Modern Science, 1300-1800* (London, 1949), p. 153.
[23] Thomas, *Montpellier*, p. 187 ff.
[24] Roland, *Mémoires*, p. 12.
[25] *Lettres de Madame Roland*, publiées par Claude Perroud, nouvelle

The lawyer Barbier's identification with the aristocracy is evident from his preoccupation with social background, and he was not above pointing out the humble provenance of many of his distinguished and arrogant colleagues at the bar: ". . . Suard, son of a solicitor, and grandson of a village tavern-keeper . . . ; Normant, son of a solicitor, and grandson of a sergeant from Tours; Aubry, son of a consulting barrister and grandson of a tailor; Fessart, son of a solicitor, and grandson of a peasant."[26] Barbier was very much agitated, further-more, by a militia ordinance in 1747, which unlike previous such ordinances, did *not* exempt the wealthier merchants. This meant that "the son of a wealthy wholesale merchant, brought up in easy circumstances and well-educated, would be included on the same list as his father's valet, and as servants, workers, and boys from the shops . . . [etc.]. . . . This is humiliating and difficult, and one might say that it is too much so."[27]

As a matter of fact, feelings ran very high among the bour-geois on this subject of their obligation to serve, as *roturiers*, in the socially stigmatized militia, and the merchants whom Barbier spoke of would gladly have paid large taxes for the exemption of their sons from service.[28] Both the *négociants* and the intendant of La Rochelle in 1775 appealed to the government, on more or less the same grounds, for militia exemption for the sons of these *négociants*. The *négociants* pleaded that subjection to the *tirage* was incompatible with the education they prided themselves on giving their sons, and that it was also incompatible with the possibility of en-noblement held out (in an edict of 1767) by the king to the most distinguished merchants.[29] The intendant also argued

série 1767-1780 (Paris, 1913), I, p. 127; this letter was written in Febru-ary 1773.

[26] Barbier, *Chronique*, I, p. 58.

[27] Barbier, *Journal*, II, pp. 353-354.

[28] *Ibid.*, II, p. 357. M.-A. Robbe, "Les milices dans l'intendance de la Flandre wallonne au 18e siècle," *Revue du Nord*, XXIII (1937), pp. 5-50, shows the unfair incidence of militia service.

[29] Garnault, *Le commerce rochelais*, I, pp. 54-55.

against the humiliation of these young men, many of whom were destined for the nobility.[30] It was the pride of the would-be or near-aristocrat that was at stake. Although the bourgeois of the 18th century built his expectations of social mobility on implicitly universalist values, there is little or no expression of egalitarianism.[31] Careers should be open to talent, but these successful careers were only means to the end of nobility, not ends in themselves: once noble status had been achieved, the occupational function embodied in the career became of secondary importance, indeed, it was best forgotten.

Only in the dramatic literature of the period do we find indications of sentiments about the equal dignity of human beings regardless of their social position, and even here, as we shall see, the authors bowed almost unconsciously to the aristocratic prejudices of the time. The plays that are relevant here presented the merchant in a new, more favorable light, and they dealt frequently with the triumph of romantic love over class barriers. In more general terms, the drama of the 18th century did lend a new dignity to the bourgeoisie; it dealt seriously and sympathetically with the problems of everyday life, the hopes and fears experienced in the home and on the job, instead of, as in the 17th century, being preoccupied with the lives of classical and historical heroes. Eighteenth century drama was aimed at the sentiments, or rather the sentimentality, of a predominantly bourgeois audience, which preferred the pathos of domestic disaster with a happy ending to the deeper tragic conflicts of classical drama.

The *négociants* assumed a new stature and dignity in drama, whether they rose from nothing and were self-made by dint of hard work—like, for example, Dominique in Mercier's *Brouette du Vinaigrier*—or whether, as in Beaumarchais' *Les*

---

[30] *Ibid.*, I, p. 58.

[31] This does not mean that there was no resentment of specific noble privileges. But the elimination of these privileges was generally seen as constituting not the "conditions of equality" (cf. Carré, *La noblesse*, p. 313), but rather the conditions for limited mobility.

*Deux Amis* and Sedaine's *Philosophe sans le savoir*, they were really noblemen and "have, indeed, only heightened merit for professing proudly their esteem for an occupation against which there was still so much prejudice."[32] The merchants of these 18th century dramas are no longer the ridiculous and insecure *bourgeois gentilshommes* of Molière's day; they have a certain self-respect, and in Destouches' plays even a kind of pride in their class status. This pride in bourgeois class status is not unequivocal, however; it is usually mixed with strong positive sentiments toward noble status. The merchant Brice, in La Chaussée's *L'Homme de Fortune*, is "serene in the consciousness of the dignity of his class, and refused a ready-made family-tree from a professional genealogist." Yet Brice does not despise, he rather respects the nobility.[33] Mme. Duru, in Voltaire's *La femme qui a raison*, is a lady who tries to buy socially advantageous marriages for her children, ostensibly because they are good investments, but we suspect that in strictly economic terms, at least, there were better investments available.

The culmination of the supposed rehabilitation of the merchant in the characters of Sedaine's Vanderk (in *Le philosophe sans le savoir*) and Beaumarchais' Aurelly (*Les deux amis*), the finest and most dignified merchants on the 18th century French stage, is, nevertheless not free of the same ambivalences about the fundamental dignity of commerce. The crucial fact about these two characters, who extol and exemplify the virtues of commerce, is, from our point of view, that both are *pseudo-bourgeois*, that they are really noblemen. (Vanderk is of the old *noblesse*, and is engaging in commerce in spite of this; Aurelly is more recently ennobled and is continuing in his occupation of merchant.) Their vindication of commerce, therefore, is the more convincing for their being

[32] Félix Gaiffe, *Etude sur le drame du 18e siècle* (Paris, 1910), pp. 370-371.
[33] Walter T. Peirce, *The Bourgeois from Molière to Beaumarchais: the Study of a Dramatic Type* (Columbus, Ohio, 1907), p. 66.

noblemen and represents, perhaps, an attempt by the authors to have the best of both the bourgeois and the noble worlds. Commerce, it is implied, has dignity in *anyone's* hands if he is honest, but it still requires the sanction of the nobleman to enhance and insure its acceptability. Though he has gained in self-respect and in the respect of his creators, the bourgeois merchant in drama is not yet self-sufficient as bourgeois.

When we come to the treatment of the subject of *mésalliance* in drama, we find a curiously similar situation. Many of the 18th century authors we have mentioned sense the universalistic implications in the triumph of romantic love, or the respect for virtue, over class differences. In several plays, such as Sedaine's *Félix*, or Marivaux' *Jeu de l'amour et du hasard*, or in Voltaire's *Nanine*, the attractive qualities of personal virtue (rather than physical beauty, apparently, at this time) triumph over the handicap of lowly birth. But the significant thing about these plays by Sedaine and Marivaux, and others by the same authors, is that the characters, whose simple virtue appears to triumph, turn out in the end *to have been noble all the time*, either without their own knowledge, as was Felix, or deliberately in disguise, as were those in *Le jeu de l'amour et du hasard*. Only Voltaire's Nanine undergoes no such metamorphosis. The ultimate desirability of noble birth seems to be given recognition in this roundabout fashion.

An outright attack on the nobility as an institution was unusual in dramatic literature. Gresset in *Le Méchant* or Saurin in *Les moeurs du temps* compared noble morality unfavorably with bourgeois morality;[34] the noble characters lack *honnêteté* and they are incapable of true affection, but their *raison d'être* is not questioned. In some of Marivaux's dramas there are more genuinely egalitarian implications, especially in the *Ile des esclaves*, in which Trivelin, the ruler of the island, says: "Differences in social status are nothing but a way the gods

---

[34] Léon Fontaine, *Le théâtre et la philosophie au 18e siècle* (Versailles, 1878), p. 181.

have of testing us."[35] And the classic expression of these sentiments, which did indeed become stronger and more widespread in the 1780's, is found in Figaro's soliloquy:

"Because you are a great seigneur, you think you are a great genius! . . . Nobility, wealth, high rank, offices, all that makes one so proud! What have you done to deserve all these advantages? You gave yourself the trouble to be born, and nothing more. General opinion to the contrary, you are a pretty ordinary man. . . ."[36]

Bourgeois drama, then, shares the values of 18th century French society. For one thing, the bourgeois had gained, perforce, a certain amount of recognition in society, and this recognition is mirrored in the frequent preoccupation of dramatists with "bourgeois" themes, appealing to the growing bourgeois audience. But more important, the prevalence of mobile bourgeois in these plays, and especially of bourgeois seeking nobility or of noble merchants, seems to indicate that the dramas reflect the contradictions and conflicts in the class attitudes both of their literary creators and of the bourgeois class as a whole, whether fictitious or real. And it is worth noting that the ambivalence in bourgeois class attitudes between adherence to the traditional system and the expectation of mobility which was based on universalistic values rarely led to any such explicit rejection of the aristocratic ideal as is found in Beaumarchais.

Class attitudes, like the ones we have discussed above, may or may not find direct expression in political terms. To a certain extent, of course, political institutions are necessarily related to the same values that underlie the class structure, and they are therefore correlated with it. For example, the open class system, which approves of mobility, and democratic

[35] P. C. de Chamblain de Marivaux, *L'île des esclaves* (*Oeuvres Complètes*, v), (Paris, 1781), p. 65.

[36] P. A. C. de Beaumarchais, *La folle journée, ou le mariage de Figaro* (*Oeuvres complètes*, ii), (Paris, 1809), Act IV, scene iii.

political institutions both rest on universalistic and rational values, while a class system nearer the caste end of the continuum and political aristocracy have a certain congruence based on particularistic and traditional values. The general endorsement of the legitimacy of existing political authorities is interdependent, therefore, with sentiments about the justice of the stratification system. In an aristocratic society, in which political activity is hereditarily ascribed to a small elite in the society, endorsement of the legitimacy of authority is passive, and the "mass apathy" which is problematic in a democracy is institutionalized.[37] When, however, the justice of the class system is called into question, such discontent may be expressed in demands for remedy by the political authorities or in demands for the reallocation of authority itself, for "reform" or "revolution."

Just as any rejection of the traditional class system was a rare occurrence among the bourgeois of the 18th century, so also was any real alienation from the existing political institutions. The bourgeoisie accepted the aristocracy's feudal preemption of political authority, at least until the very last years of the *ancien régime*, though earlier there might be murmurs against the actual conduct of affairs or against the actual holders of various offices. Men might be fallible, even kings might be so, but the offices were hallowed by God and by tradition. It is one of the most important contributions of Mornet's monumental *Les origines intellectuelles de la Révolution française* to show how little of the alienation from traditional views that did occur before the 1780's was explicitly formulated in political terms with revolutionary significance.

It is almost a truism, too, that up until 1770, at least, most of the intellectuals, like Voltaire or Montesquieu, were still sufficiently pessimistic about human nature to doubt the feasibility of popular self-government, and tried to compromise between their rational values and their traditional faith in

[37] B. Barber, *"Mass Apathy" and Voluntary Social Participation in the United States*, unpublished Ph.D. thesis, Harvard University, 1949, Part II.

aristocracy by recommending some form of "enlightened des-
potism" or constitutional monarchy. In part, of course, this
distrust of popular democracy was based not so much on attitudes hostile to social mobility as on the conviction that
only an intellectual aristocracy could maximize the efficiency
of government by the rational understanding of social laws.
Likewise, the impatience of the business classes with the administrative and legal institutions of the Old Regime, which
found expression finally in the *cahiers* of 1789, was directed
not so much against the traditional bases of these institutions,
as against the irrational and incalculable confusion they caused,
which hindered efficient business operations. For a long time,
few intellectuals or businessmen were willing to face the extreme egalitarian implications of their rationalism and of their
utilitarian conception of a "science of morals and legislation."

The acceptance by the bourgeoisie of the political as well as
the class system of 18th century France is shown by their lack
of interest, their mass apathy, as far as politics are concerned.
Inactivity in the political field was expected of them, and, on
the whole, they conformed gladly to this expected pattern.
They sought political authority incidentally, perhaps, in their
major quest for ennoblement, but often these political offices
were only honorary, anyway (see Chapter VI), and in general
the bourgeoisie took very little interest in the world of politics in which they had no legitimate share. Barbier clearly
showed his negative attitude toward any political activism. In
discussing the petition of some fifty lawyers against royal
execution of the bull *Unigenitus*, directed against Jansenism,
Barbier said: "Fortunately neither my father nor I are mixed
up with that list of fifty. I think one should do one's job
honorably, without interfering in affairs of State over which
one has neither power nor authority."[38]

The lawyers were, in fact, almost the only bourgeois who
were drawn into political controversy at all, by their involve-
ment in the conflict between king and Parlement, and, if Bar-

[38] Barbier, *Chronique*, II, p. 32.

bier is at all typical, they were drawn in reluctantly. On occasion, the *esprit de corps* of the whole bar forced these lawyers into action critical of the royal policy against the Jansenists and the Parlement, and whenever this happened, men like Marais and Barbier were quick to protest their loyalty to the king in spite of his misguided policy. Sometimes, by appealing directly to the king as the highest authority, against some abuse of which he was presumably ignorant, the lawyers made sure of the evidence of their loyalty while attempting to protect their interests.[39] Marais was usually able to resist even this temptation,[40] but Hardy declared that his distress at the banishment of Parlement was in no way in conflict with his complete and devoted loyalty to his "royal master," or with his agreement with the "most important people of the State."[41] Barbier, also, felt that no limitation should be placed on the monarchy, and he opposed the tactics of the critical lawyers: "when one knows, or should know, that the king can of right make anyone keep silent and obey by a single word, one should not annoy the sovereign by constantly opposing his wishes, nor should one declare oneself in Paris as a constitutionally established power that may counter-balance the sovereign."[42]

Both contemporary writers and later historians have commented on this political inactivity on the part of the bourgeoisie. Sebastian Mercier complained, as always, about the frivolity of the Paris bourgeois and his political apathy: "He has fallen in the last hundred years into a kind of heedlessness about his political interests. . . ."[43] Historians like Lacroix and Taine both speak of the passivity and indifference of the bourgeois in politics.[44] Informally and indirectly, of course, the

[39] *Ibid.*, p. 132.
[40] Marais, *Mémoires*, "Introduction" by Lescure, I, p. 43.
[41] Hardy, *Mes loisirs*, p. 296.
[42] Barbier, *Journal*, III, p. 428.
[43] Louis-Sebastien Mercier, *Tableau de Paris*, nouvelle édition augmentée (Amsterdam, 1783), I, p. 31.
[44] Lacroix, *18e siècle*, pp. 61-62; H. Taine, *Les origines de la France contemporaine. L'ancien régime* (Paris, 1898), p. 400.

bourgeoisie had wielded political power from the time of its beginning in the later Middle Ages, since the monarchy had depended on bourgeois support in the form of bourgeois wealth in its struggle against the nobility; and we shall see in a later chapter what advantages accrued to the bourgeoisie from this alliance. The bourgeoisie had also, especially in the 16th and 17th centuries, contributed important ministers to the state. But in the 18th century, at least, the bourgeois-in-the-street minded his own business as far as politics was concerned.

There was, of course, dissatisfaction with the *ancien régime*, but except for the Parlements, no one made an active political stand against the regime. What criticism there was, focused to a large extent on the maldistribution of wealth and the corruption and inequity of the taxation system—not on political privilege but rather on financial injustice. Barbier was extremely indignant, for him, when *M. le garde des sceaux* d'Armenonville and his son received 36,000 and 20,000 livres in pensions respectively: "One takes away the life annuities from 100 poor families who depended on them for their subsistence, and which were acquired by efforts for which the King is indebted, and of which there are no more reserves; one gives 56,000 livres in pensions to people who have held high offices, in which they have accumulated considerable fortunes at the expense of the people; . . . and this so that they may sit back and do nothing. Is it possible to think of anything less reasonable?"[45]

The young Mme. Roland was disgusted at the contrast between the "Asiatic splendor" with which royalty celebrated any occasion, and the "misery and . . . abjection of the brutalized people," who applauded these extravagances of their idols though they paid for them.[46] During the Regency period, Barbier felt that the regent was very wrong to give a splendid feast in honor of his mistress, when everyone was suffering from the crash after the Law fiasco: "it was

---

[45] Barbier, *Chronique*, II, p. 16.
[46] Roland, *Mémoires*, p. 93.

contrary to any human kindness to have such a feast at a time when everyone is ruined, when no one has a cent. . . ."[47]

By 1751, Barbier's concern about the great economic inequalities had led him close to questioning hereditary fiscal privileges; he recommended some kind of proportional taxation on everyone in France, as it existed in England.[48] Barbier almost certainly did not consider that a sudden attack on one such hereditary privilege as the exemption of the nobility from taxation might lead to a more general attack on all hereditary social privileges. And other such attacks on the unjust distribution of the tax burden were also, for the most part, reformist rather than revolutionary in intention. It seemed possible to remedy these social injustices, which were only partly understood because of socially trained blindness to them, by borrowing political institutions from England or Holland, without changing the essential character of French society.

Before 1770, Mornet finds only few and isolated predictions of a revolution, in the writings of d'Argenson, Mopinot, and Barbier, but Barbier, as Mornet points out, was a fearful man, who permitted his anxiety about the controversy between king and Parlement to lead his imagination to actual revolution.[49] It was not until the decade before the Revolution that the increasingly acute financial plight of the Royal Treasury made the bourgeoisie translate its discontent at "mismanagement" by individuals into a wholesale rejection of the political, economic, and social basis of a regime which fostered such mismanagement. Not till then did men like Siéyès de-

[47] Barbier, *Chronique*, I, pp. 144-145.

[48] Barbier, *Journal*, III, p. 171; the opinions of the fearful and peace-loving Barbier on such a subject are, we feel, more revealing than those of a more politically oriented person might be. Just two years previously to this, in 1749, the government itself, under Machault, had sought to introduce a tax of a twentieth on all Frenchmen without exemption, but this scheme was shattered by noble and clerical opposition. (See H. Carré, *Le règne de Louis XV 1715-1774*, in E. Lavisse, ed., *Histoire de France* [Paris, 1909], VIII, part 2, pp. 229-237.) Increasingly, such intransigeance on the part of the privileged classes must have provoked frustration and alienation on the part of the bourgeoisie.

[49] Barbier, *Journal*, IV, p. 456.

mand for the bourgeoisie authority commensurate with its economic power and its other abilities. Before that, the bourgeoisie had accepted the traditional political institutions and the legitimacy of their exclusion from them. It took the outright failure of the Old Regime to mobilize the latent hostility which was for a long time the less important component of the ambivalent bourgeois attitudes toward French society.

# CHAPTER V

## The Bourgeois Way of Life

IN any society, different classes are identifiable by their different ways of life. To the observer, that is, the many different kinds of behavior that go on within the same society are symbolic of membership in one or another of the classes of which the society is made up. The kinds of behavior that may be symbolically significant in this way are innumerable, but a few examples of the more important ones will indicate what patterns of activity are most often involved here: clothing, speech, family life, education, an appropriate occupation, food, or recreation—all serve to symbolize membership in a particular social class, apart from any other function they may have. The symbolic function of occupations may be illustrated by recalling the prestige of a military as compared to a mercantile career in pre-Revolutionary France; and as for speech, the "Oxford accent" has traditionally been associated with the English upper classes; in American society, the kind of car a man drives or the kind of fur coat his wife wears are important guides to social behavior. Even minimal clues tell us necessary things we need to know in dealing with friends and especially with strangers. Veblen may have thought that only the "leisure class" needed its symbols of success, but we now know that the phenomenon of "conspicuous consumption," in this more generalized form, is common to all societies.

The behavior of a particular class will not only serve to identify the class, but also it will be an expression of social attitudes. The class system in its more dynamic aspect—the attitudes of the members of the society towards social mobility—will be reflected in the styles of life of the several classes, and especially in the differences between them. The belief in the fundamental equality of all members of the society and

in their right to equality of opportunity will be expressed in
a different way in the styles of life from the disapproval of
social mobility and the hereditary segregation of functions. In
American society, for example, differences in styles of dress
are minimized, and only a sophisticated eye can tell a dress
from Gimbel's from one purchased at Bergdorf Goodman's;
and only the initiated know that while "everyone" has a car,
a DeSoto outranks a Chevrolet.[1] In the *ancien régime* in
France, which came nearer to being a caste society, distinctions
were explicitly approved, and symbolic differentiation of dress
was very clearly in evidence. Sometimes it was even confirmed
by law, as in the case of the legally exclusive right of the
nobility to wear both a sword and fur. Fabrics and even colors
to be used in dress were allocated on the basis of class status.

Besides exemplifying class attitudes, styles of life also express religious values. They vary in accordance with religious
definitions of right and proper conduct, with important con-
victions about the general worth-whileness of earthly goods
and of earthly success, or about the purpose and significance
of wealth or knowledge. The "this-worldly asceticism" of the
wealthy Calvinist bourgeois affected his way of life in a different way from the religion of the wealthy Catholic; the
latter could more easily segregate monastic asceticism from lay
worldliness. In an integrated society, the religious and the
social class attitudes will be congruent with one another;
that is, they will not make conflicting demands on the individual; also, in an integrated society, any set of class attitudes
will be internally consistent. For the mobile bourgeois of the
18th century, however, two kinds of conflict existed: a conflict between his attitudes as a bourgeois and his religious
values, and also an ambivalence within his class attitudes toward social mobility.

The 18th century witnessed a considerable change in the

---

[1] On this subject see B. Barber and L. Lobel, " 'Fashion' in Women's
Clothes and the American Social System," *Social Forces*, XXXI (Dec. 1952),
pp. 124-131.

ways of life of all the classes of France, a change which brought these conflicting pressures to bear on the bourgeois. Before the 18th century, the allocation of symbols of status was much more rigidly determined on the basis of the traditional class status of a particular family. During the 18th century men still reminisced about former times when "no bourgeois ever . . ." did thus and so. The nobility had formerly preempted luxurious living, artistic and literary cultivation, and, by the 17th century especially, a life that was predominantly idle. The functions traditionally allocated to the nobility—military and especially political—were now being filled by others, and so decorative idleness almost became synonymous with "vivre noblement." The bourgeoisie, on the other hand, was traditionally characterized by being hard-working, "sober," and frugal. But in the 18th century, the great increase in wealth among certain groups in the bourgeoisie increased the pressure that the socially ambitious bourgeois felt toward assimilation to the noble way of life by the manipulation of the various status-conferring symbols. More and more, the upper bourgeoisie, particularly, aimed at the acquisition of those symbols of noble status which came within its financial reach, while the middle bourgeoisie had rather more divided loyalties between the old bourgeois style of life and the noble style which was compatible with its mobility aspirations.

The ambivalences in the religious and class attitudes of the bourgeoisie that we have already discussed come clearly to the surface when we study the bourgeois way of life. To be a successful bourgeois at all meant making important compromises with the other-worldly orientation prescribed by the Catholic religion. These compromises the bourgeois businessman made. He shifted his attention to this world, and he assumed new responsibilities and set himself new goals. To carry out these new aims, it was only *rational*, of course, for the bourgeois to live simply. Luxurious consumption was incompatible with the financial demands of successful business operations and, further, such consumption too often ran the risk of inviting spoliation by the government. But in sober and frugal living the French bourgeois also found a way of easing the strain of his defection from traditional Catholic other-worldliness. The Church itself came to recognize the bourgeois's sober and conscientious devotion to his worldly affairs as a proper way to insure the salvation of his soul. For the bourgeois, the attainment of virtue came to be defined in terms of his ability to resist the worldly temptations of wealth.[2]

Far more than the Calvinist bourgeois, the French bourgeois came, ultimately, to compromise the moral and rational prescriptions for an ascetic way of life. The sober bourgeois was profoundly attracted by the noble way of life, and he was less deeply concerned with the problem of his salvation. Both the Calvinist and the Catholic bourgeois became more and more secularized, but while for the Calvinist this-worldly asceticism remained a driving force even in the secularized capitalist, the secularized French bourgeois shed his religious interests far more completely in his quest for social salvation in the form of nobility. The struggle that these French bourgeois experienced in the process of their secularization shows not only in their reflections about religion but in the ways they sought and symbolized social mobility. Once again, we find every bourgeois caught in the dilemma between acceptance of the traditional social and religious order, and rejection of that order insofar as it defined his place in it as fixed.

The fundamental problem of finding a way of life that was morally as well as socially acceptable was shared by all members of the mobile bourgeoisie, but there were variant solutions to this problem within the bourgeois class, and therefore different ways of life. The whole bourgeois class shared in fact, only one important pattern in its several ways of life, and that was its devotion to family life. To be sure, in the noble class, where the most important criterion of status was membership in a traditionally noble family, lineage and family

<hr />

[2] Groethuysen, *Buergerliche Welt- und Lebensanschauung*, II, pp. 70, 76.

connections were of great significance; and also, when the fief and other property became *de facto* hereditary, this connection of family and property increased the importance of children, and especially male children, to a noble father. But where the noble concern for the family had to do with pride and property, the bourgeois attitude constituted all this and more besides. To the bourgeois, domesticity or life *in the home* with his family had greater emotional significance than it did for the nobility. Physical well-being in the home was very important, and any threats to its physical safety were resented.[3] In bourgeois homes, harmony and affection between members of the family, between husbands and wives, and between parents and children, were ideals and reality. Man and wife "lived together and did not blush for it, while in the nobility man and wife pretended to live separately, at least in public."[4] From this emphasis on conjugal happiness it was only a step, made in the course of the Revolution, which brought the general acceptance of bourgeois values, to the identification of virtue with pre-marital chastity and marital fidelity. Glotz, in discussing the qualities of the hostesses of salons, speaks of their moral authority, which "in the 18th century . . . is not conferred by virtue in the sense of chastity. There was much talk of virtue at that time, but it meant disinterestedness and generosity, an eloquent concern for the public welfare. The word never had that narrow and somewhat overscrupulous sense that the 19th century gave it. One had to wait for the substitution of bourgeois for aristocratic morality before such a high price was attached to good morals, to respectability."[5] But even before the Revolution enthroned "middle class respectability," in all its aspects, the bourgeoisie disapproved of the lax sexual morality for which the 18th century nobility was famous.

Among the 18th century bourgeois, the older ideal of the

---

[3] Roustan, *Les philosophes*, pp. 233-234.
[4] Lacroix, *18e siècle*, p. 66.
[5] Marguerite Glotz, *Salons du 18e siècle* (Paris, 1945), pp. 14-15.

stern parent changed to that of the loving, if not doting, parent. Friendship rather than authority relations developed between parents and children.[6] Vanel observes that whenever there were exceptions in Caen to the strict obedience relationship between parents and children, they occurred among the bourgeoisie.[7] Barbier revealed the association contemporaries made between close family ties and the bourgeois way of life when he noted, in 1750, the welcome given by the king to two of the royal princesses at Fontainebleau: "The king kissed them, first one, then the other, for a quarter of an hour, crying *like a good Parisian bourgeois head of the family*."[8]

This new emphasis on the importance of the family and on affectionate ties between parents and children was evident in both 18th century drama and art. Children of all ages figured prominently in many of the bourgeois dramas, "and simply enumerating the titles of the plays of Florian (*The Good Father, The Good Mother, The Happy Household, The Good Son*), is more revealing than any analysis or any number of quotations."[9] Marriage and family life were romanticized in plays by Mercier, Diderot, and Dejaube. After 1730, especially, the tyrannous parent familiar in the plays of Molière, Dancourt, and Regnard disappeared, and the new pattern consisted of affectionate parents, dutiful sons, and the *cri du sang*. In Voltaire's *Enfant Prodigue* (1736), the bourgeois father had great tenderness even for his scape-grace son; parental love is the central theme in several of La Chaussée's *comédies larmoyantes*.[10] Affection and family bliss pervade the paintings of Greuze and Chardin.

Ties of affection bound not only an individual's immediate family, but also the more extended family group. Besnard remembers that in his childhood in Doué he and his family were on terms of "cousinship" with almost everyone in the town,

[6] Babeau, *Les bourgeois*, pp. 301-302.
[7] Vanel, *La vie publique à Caen*, p. 49.
[8] Barbier, *Journal*, III, pp. 176-177; our italics.
[9] Gaiffe, *Etude sur le drame*, p. 268.
[10] Peirce, *From Molière to Beaumarchais*, p. 52 ff.

and everyone was greeted as "cousin" in the streets, however remote the kinship tie. There was much visiting back and forth among these many relatives,[11] in fact, visiting was one of the most important forms of bourgeois recreation. Bourgeois leisure activities became increasingly associated with the home, since the bourgeois began to find it degrading to attend popular open air festivities.[12] In the small town of Tulle, as in Doué, entertainment was restricted almost wholly to visiting among a small circle of relatives and friends; "social obligations" extended no further than that.[13]

But the emphasis on family life was the *one* aspect of the bourgeois way of life which cut across all its sub-groups, and as soon as we speak, for example, of patterns of recreation and entertainment we touch on areas in which the variations within the bourgeois class were immense. The lawyer in a small town like Doué for whom recreation meant quiet inter-family visiting, and the Parisian financier who required the most lavish entertainment, lived in two different and hostile worlds, and even among the Parisian bourgeoisie there were many styles of life. These styles range along a continuum, from great simplicity and austerity at one end to extreme luxury at the other, and the many points on the continuum between the two extremes show the progressive compromises made by the mobile bourgeois between the "old" bourgeois sobriety and the lure of the symbols of noble status.

The "old" bourgeoisie, composed of merchants, doctors, and lawyers, were well-to-do if not wealthy people, whose way of life can be described by such terms as simplicity, sobriety, and industry. The frequent designation of this group as *old* bourgeoisie derived from the fact that both their social and economic status as bourgeois was of relatively long standing, and was, therefore, in striking contrast to the status and wealth of the financiers, who were, rightly or wrongly, gen-

[11] Besnard, *Souvenirs*, I, pp. 25-26.
[12] Babeau, *Les bourgeois*, pp. 209-211.
[13] Fage, *La vie à Tulle*, pp. 255-256.

erally thought of as the "nouveaus riche."[14] This group held most tenaciously to the old bourgeois style of life, to which, in part at least, it owed its slow social rise. Their full approval was given to simple and frugal living. Besnard wrote in his *Souvenirs* that in Doué in the mid-18th century any luxury was entirely reserved for great seigneurs and a few very wealthy merchants.[15] Barbier wrote approvingly about a M. de Laverdy, a controller of finances: "Much has been said about M. de Laverdy's frugality and modest living. He and his wife had an income of at most 16,000 livres. They lived piously and in the bourgeois manner; the ways of the Court did not suit them."[16] M. Grosley went so far as to call sobriety the very fountain of youth for both body and soul of the bourgeoisie.[17]

The puritanical orderliness, frugality, and industry of some of the large commercial houses are remarked by Babeau.[18] He describes the house of Bethman at Bordeaux, where everyone worked from 6 a.m. till 8 p.m. and went right to bed after dinner; or the house of Texier, also at Bordeaux: "In spite of his wealth, the country house where Texier entertained his friends was more remarkable for its cleanliness than for its luxury. One did not play there; but one lived there very happily, without being niggardly or prodigal."[19] From the legal profession, too, we find examples that show that not only moderately successful men like Barbier or Marais but even some of the most eminent lawyers of the time maintained the simple style of life (though this was not true of all of them). Cochin, one of the greatest Paris lawyers of the century, lived in style that was in sharp contrast with that

[14] The wealth of many financiers, e.g., the Boullongnes, was not really "new," but it increased so rapidly in a comparatively short period of time as to create that impression. See Caix de Saint-Aymon, *Une famille d'artisan et de financiers du 17e et 18e siècle. Les Boullognes* (Paris, 1914).

[15] Besnard, *Souvenirs*, I, p. 218.

[16] Barbier, *Journal*, IV, p. 480.

[17] Grosley, *Vie de M. Grosley* (Londres, 1787), p. 49.

[18] Babeau, *Les bourgeois*, p. 65 ff.

[19] *Ibid.*, p. 66.

of his great rival Le Normand: "Cochin was as modest as his rival was boisterous and superb. . . . He was simple in his private life, religious, even somewhat jansenist."[20] Another fine "old" bourgeois lawyer, Barthélemy d'Orbanne of Grenoble, refused the office of counselor in the Parlement because it was incompatible with his simple way of life.[21]

Besides sobriety and austerity, thrift—the elimination of waste and the preoccupation with saving money—was another cardinal commandment of the bourgeois way of life. In part, this was an occupational necessity; it was "good business." The merchant could not "waste" excess income on luxurious consumption, but must add it to productive capital to expand the earning power of his enterprise. But the bourgeois felt that careful economy was more than just a rational prescription; it was also a moral duty and a way of indicating the fact that, for better or worse, a man *was* a bourgeois and had a serious and honest purpose in the world. Sombart sees this economy as one of the most important virtues peculiar to the bourgeois, "not thrift imposed by necessity, by want, but thrift conceived as a virtue."[22] Such thrift in the use of resources was the very opposite of the noble attitude towards his patrimony; the nobleman spent up to the hilt and tried only, as best he could, to keep out of debt. Séras felt that before there was ever any possibility of a *noblesse commerçante* in France (which he doubted, anyway) it would be necessary to convince the nobility of the necessary qualifications of the merchant: "One must not conceal from the nobility that vehement desires, the taste for frivolous amusements, are more harmful in the commercial occupation than in any other; for if on the one hand the activities of that occupation help to accumulate wealth, it demands on the other hand more restraint, preci-

---

[20] Joachim A. J. Gaudry, *Histoire du barreau de Paris depuis son origine jusqu'à 1830* (Paris, 1864), II, p. 98.

[21] Egret, *Le Parlement de Dauphiné*, II, p. 83.

[22] Werner Sombart, *Le bourgeois, contribution à l'histoire morale et intellectuelle de l'homme économique moderne* (Paris, 1926), p. 133.

sion, industry, economy, than any of those professions that the nobility can enter." The uncontrolled desires, Séras warned, would inevitably destroy what had been built up in the spirit of moderation.[23] The way of life of the proper bourgeois protected him from such disaster. The way in which the bourgeoisie was identified with thrift is amusingly illustrated in a remark by the lawyer Target, in 1787: "The state of our finances seems to be more disquieting than ever: but what remedy is there when on the occasion of some attempts by the King to economize in his own household, it is said that *he acts like a bourgeois*."[24] This was evidently no practice fit for a king of France.

The devotion of the man of the bourgeoisie to his work, which we have mentioned earlier in connection with social values, constitutes the third important component of the "old" bourgeois way of life. If the work of the bourgeois was co-ordinated in some way with the attainment of salvation, it was, too, an end in itself, and it took precedence over all other activities of this world. Even intellectual pursuits had only the status of "avocations." The bourgeois of Dijon, for example, though he might have a great interest in all kinds of studies, felt a much higher obligation to his work. The driest studies, even, were considered to be mere diversions. The well-known humanist Bouhier was always a lawyer first and an author second.[25] The long, hard hours put in by his lawyer colleagues, both young and old, were noted by Berryer,[26] and Bachaumont quoted the following comment on his doctor-grandfather by a jealous colleague: "He is a complete hypocrite, who will do anything, provided he profits from it; a melancholy, burning man, who talks only about the Virgin Mary and of scruples, and who, in every possible way, seeks

---

[23] Séras, *Le commerce ennobli*, pp. 25-26.
[24] Boulloche, *Target*, p. 47.
[25] Bouchard, *La bourgeoisie bourguignonne*, p. 485.
[26] Berryer, *Souvenir*, I, pp. 33-34.

only to increase his practice and his fortune."[27] This is not an unfamiliar caricature of the bourgeois.

When we come, now, to consider the way of life of the middle bourgeoisie more closely, we find that in addition to the traditional moral pressure toward austerity, thrift, and industry, toward the interests of business and success as a bourgeois, there were also strong pressures exerted on the mobile bourgeois away from this style of life. "Vivre noblement" and all it implied pulled the French businessman, more or less strongly, toward luxury, extravagance, and idleness. Those who resisted these latter pressures to a large extent expressed strong disapproval of the luxury-loving group, but by the 18th century few escaped this kind of "corruption" altogether.

By the 18th century, the very strict rules on how "clothes varied according to status" had been relaxed considerably. A hundred years earlier, certain kinds of cloth were used exclusively by members of certain classes: drugget by the artisan, woolen cloth by the bourgeois, and silk by the nobility. In those days, women of the high bourgeoisie might wear taffeta, but velours were reserved for noblewomen.[28] These rigid distinctions were broken down by less conservative people in the 18th century, although Taine undoubtedly exaggerates the leveling that had taken place between the classes, and the extent of symbolization of egalitarian values in dress.[29] Black and grey were still the two colors used predominantly by the *roturiers* of Laval, though some wealthy bourgeois did use bright colors: "But the old bourgeois remained faithful during a large part of the 18th century to his dark colored dress. . . ."[30] The English traveller Arthur Young objected to

[27] Louis P. de Bachaumont, *Anecdotes piquantes pour servir à histoire de la société française à la fin du règne de Louis XV* (Bruxelles, 1881), II, Appendix "Jeunesse," pp. 229-230.

[28] Vanel, *La vie publique à Caen*, p. 179.

[29] H. Taine, *Les origines de la France contemporaine. L'ancien régime* (Paris, 1898), pp. 407-408.

[30] J. M. Richard, *La vie privée dans une province de l'Ouest: Laval au 17e et 18e siècle* (Paris, 1922), p. 82.

the black clothes of persons of "moderate fortune" not so much because of the "dusky hue of this company," but "as too great a distinction"; and he thought that the "pride, arrogance and ill-temper of English wealth" would never have stood for it.[31]

French wealth also was becoming too "proud" for such humble clothing. At Doué, bright-colored hair ribbons and furbelows were worn not only by noblewomen but also by those "who by their markedly superior wealth or high profession of their husbands were distinguished from the other bourgeois families." However, wives of notaries, surgeons and retail merchants, that is, lesser bourgeois, did not permit themselves this luxury.[32] At Angers, the customs were on the whole the same, and bourgeois ladies over fifty who wore any colors were still subject to ridicule.[33] Little Manon Phlipon recalled that the bourgeois of Paris spent quite a lot of money to look his best on his Sunday afternoon walks in the Tuileries, or on such occasions as baptisms and weddings,[34] but unfortunately she did not compare this bourgeois finery with that of the nobility. The bourgeois always ran the risk of "overdressing" for his status, of meeting with censure and ridicule from his fellow-bourgeois or from the nobility. Mme. Tamisier must have been a well-dressed lady, judging by the inventory of her wardrobe, but she had been careful not to "parade a degree of luxury above that proper to her status."[35] Barbier's contempt for M. Dodun, who "had had a suit adorned with lace, no more and no less than that of an officer in the gendarmes," which was judged by all to be utterly ridiculous and made people dig up his lowly birth,[36] reveals the dangers and strains in the situation.

[31] Arthur Young, *Travels in France and Italy during the Years 1787, 1788, and 1789* (London, Toronto, New York, 1915), p. 108.

[32] Besnard, *Souvenirs*, I, p. 28.    [33] *Ibid.*, I, p. 120.

[34] Roland, *Mémoires*, pp. 19-20.

[35] O. Teissier, *La maison d'un bourgeois au 18e siècle* (Paris, 1895), p. 15.

[36] Barbier, *Chronique*, I, p. 379.

A noteworthy feature of the Tamisier household, which Teissier describes in great detail, was a sedan chair. This apparently was the hope and dream of every bourgeoise, for "while not wishing to parade any extravagance which would have been incompatible with M. Tamisier's careful ways, Mme. Tamisier was very glad to follow with moderation the current which carried the bourgeois class toward imitation of the nobility."[37] It was a strong current, and it caused difficulties and embarrassments, and even guilt feelings and recriminations. The problem of the propriety of the ownership of silver makes a nice example of bourgeois conflicts. According to Besnard, many children in Doué were *not* presented with silver goblets at birth, because their parents were afraid of being censured for social pretension,[38] but at Laval the possession of silverware was considered by the bourgeoisie to be an appropriate way of indicating "a certain social standing."[39] Mercier sneered at the bourgeois of Paris for their interest in the social value of silver: "The ambition of a bourgeois is to have flat silverware. . . . To have it means to emerge from the bourgeoisie; one makes this expenditure only in order to have the pleasure of putting ones arms on it."[40] Barbier noted in his journal in 1760 the tightening up by law on the use of coats of arms, and he remarked that this would hit a great many Paris bourgeois, for the use of the "couronne de comte" on carriages and silverware was very general, as was the wearing of swords, by those who had no real right to do so.[41] Gill-Mark shows the conflict of M. Le Page, a distinguished merchant of Rouen: "In accordance with a widespread custom among the wealthy bourgeois of that time, who were ambitious for a rapprochement with the nobility, [he] had gotten the authorization to wear arms," but in his case this was not the "forwardness of the parvenu," for he was a

[37] Teissier, *Maison d'un bourgeois*, p. 4.
[38] Besnard, *Souvenirs*, I, p. 42.      [39] Richard, *Laval*, p. 67.
[40] Quoted in Vanel, *La vie publique à Caen*, p. 106.
[41] Barbier, *Journal*, IV, p. 361.

"*négociant* highly thought of for the austerity of his habits and morals."[42]

Forms of address, both of parents and relatives, and of strangers and acquaintances, were differentiated by class in the *ancien régime*, and here too the bourgeois tried to acquire some of the appellations and titles of the noble.[43] Although the bourgeois were still given to nicknames (Jacquon, Pierrot, Manon, etc.) which were characteristic of the lower classes, they now used such expression as "mon chère père," and "ma chère mère," which were current only among the nobility and which were considered ludicrous by the artisans.[44] François Chéron recalled that his niece Marie was always "bourgeoisement" called Manette, because more elegant fashions in names were not yet current at the time.[45] Already by the 17th century, merchants in larger towns especially had acquired the title of "monsieur," even when spoken to by the nobility, instead of "maître," which was used only for artisans.[46] By the later 18th century, even women of the middle bourgeoisie of Ponthivy had ceased to sign modestly "La . . . une telle," and were now "Demoiselles."[47] The best-known ambition of the bourgeois, of course, was to acquire the *particule*. M. de Boulogne, a future *roturier* prelate, himself added this particle to his name, for no one with any ambition would dream of signing "simply Boulogne."[48] And the same ambitions prompted M. Geoffrion, a merchant of Valenciennes, to "pol-

[42] Gill-Mark, *Mme. Du Boccage*, pp. 3-4.

[43] Note that these bourgeois aspirations are a far cry from the revolutionary appellation of "citoyen," inspired by egalitarian ideals, and from the universal use of "mister" in American society.

[44] Besnard, *Souvenirs*, 1, p. 56.

[45] Hervé-Bazin, "Récits inédits de François Chéron sur la vie de famille dans les classes bourgeoises avant la Révolution," *Revue de l'Anjou*, 11 (1881), p. 68.

[46] Babeau, *Les bourgeois*, pp. 73-74.

[47] F. L. Lay, *Histoire de la ville et communauté de Ponthivy au 18e siècle* (Paris, 1911), p. 48.

[48] Abbé Alphonse Delacroix, *M. de Boulogne, archévêque de Troyes* (Paris, 1886), p. 12.

ish up his only too evident status as *roturier* by adding to his name that of the fief of Volouris."[49]

The number of really elaborate bourgeois town houses was small in the 18th century. Besnard recalled that in Angers, in the latter half of the century, there was hardly a private home remarkable either for size or exterior appearance. The first one was built while he lived there. Even the wealthiest families lived in relatively small houses and crowded several beds into one room. In Doué, where he lived in his youth, there were only two "better" homes, which were distinguished by greater elegance and cleanliness.[50] At Troyes, though, and also at Dijon, the richest merchants did build huge houses. At Marseilles the Borelli had such a house, at Bordeaux the wine merchant Bethman, and at Abbeville the Van Robais.[51] And the wealthiest financiers, as we shall see, laid a very high premium on the building of magnificent mansions. But even the modest-living old bourgeois had one luxury very close to his heart when it came to housing, and this was a country house.[52] A great many of the bourgeois families at Doué had country houses and "châteaux" at a greater or lesser distance from town, and they hastened to go there whenever business permitted. On holidays, the town became a desert.[53] The men of the time loved nature; their country homes were simply furnished, and general informality was customary there. Also, of course, it was the fashion to go to the country, and the bourgeois no longer ignored such "fashions."[54]

One of the clearest illustrations of the attraction of the aristocratic way of life for the "old-fashioned" bourgeois is the appeal that early retirement had for them. For all their devotion to hard work, the bourgeois did not shrink at retirement; they certainly did not feel the great anxiety at the no-

[49] Legros, "Dépenses d'un bourgeois," pp. 212-213.
[50] Besnard, *Souvenirs*, I, pp. 119, 14.
[51] Babeau, *Les bourgeois*, p. 55 ff.
[52] Vanel, *La vie publique à Caen*, p. 113.
[53] Besnard, *Souvenirs*, I, p. 127.
[54] Babeau, *Les bourgeois*, p. 213 ff.

tion of retirement that many American businessmen are said to feel. Unless a merchant had an unusual desire for wealth, he would most often retire early, either to an honorific office or simply to a life of leisure; especially in those towns where commercial rivalry was not too strong, "the merchants rested as soon as they had amassed sufficient money to assure a comfortable existence."[55] Besnard confirmed this in his description of life in Doué: "Men retired gladly from business when they had an income of 3 or 4,000 livres, which was considered at that time in the Third Estate to be a very respectable fortune; and it was at that time the generally accepted opinion that whoever could not live on 3,000 livres could not live on 10,000 either."[56] This was, after all, not Calvinist this-worldly asceticism.

For the middle bourgeois, however, the gradual adaptation to a more luxurious way of life concomitant with upward mobility was problematic, and he had some guilt feelings about it. It was perhaps because of these very guilt feelings that the middle bourgeois reacted so negatively to the luxurious living of the financial bourgeoisie who had no apparent hesitations about extravagance and luxury. Even mobility itself had only limited approval, and so striking a social success as that of the financiers aroused many sentiments about social pretension and presumption. It did not seem "right" to many that money could now apparently buy everything, from seats to the opera to servants.[57] Barbier was outraged when a M. Le Prêtre, the nephew of a receiver general, took his new bride to the opera: "Since it is the custom to go to the opera the first Friday after being married, especially among the nobility, those people were there, with many diamonds, in the first box next to the Queen's, a box usually reserved for titled and noble people. But such is today's *luxury* and *im-*

---

[55] Babeau, *Les bourgeois*, pp. 72-73; here we see again the difficulty of keeping the businessman in business.

[56] Besnard, *Souvenirs*, I, pp. 129-130.

[57] Duclos, *Mémoires sécrétes*, pp. 3-4.

*pertinence*: it is sufficient to be rich in order to pretend to be great."[58]

It was *nouveau-riche* presumption rather than just luxury that Barbier was attacking here, though great luxury itself was often shocking and outrageous to the "bon bourgeois." M. Hardy, the old-fashioned gentleman mentioned before, was full of shocked disapproval, for example, at a bourgeois wedding carried out in great style: "In order to transmit to posterity an example of the ostentation of the bourgeoisie of this century, I thought I had better insert here a small detail about the crazy expenditures made on the occasion of the marriage celebrated here today between . . . the oldest son of sieur Trudon, a dealer in groceries who has in the village of Antony, near Paris, a famous candle factory, and who lives in Paris, and Mlle. Jouanne. . . ." Hardy remarked that the girl's dowry was 80,000 livres; he catalogued all her expensive gifts and described the elegance of the wedding banquet, comparing it to one held at the marriage of none less than the Duke of Chartres to Mlle. de Penthièvre.[59] Even Mme. d'Epinay, brought up in a fairly well-to-do bourgeois home, was shocked when she first came to Epinay and found "all that the most refined, and I dare say the most indecent luxury might conceive of in the way of useless and nevertheless pleasant things."[60]

Among the bourgeois intellectuals of the period, we find various attitudes towards luxury, all of which were influenced by the new "lay morality." Voltaire justified luxury by its benefits to the total economy of the country and by its contributions to the gracious living of men like himself. In economic terms, he thought,

> "The wealthy man is born to spend a lot,
> The poor man is made that he may save a lot."[16]

[58] Barbier, *Journal*, III, p. 160; our italics.
[59] Hardy, *Mes loisirs*, p. 142.     [60] D'Epinay, *Mémoires*, p. 322.
[61] Voltaire, *Défense du Mondain*:
> "Le riche est né pour beaucoup depenser;
> Le pauvre est fait pour beaucoup amasser."

and in less general terms he felt that ". . . for a bourgeois of Paris or London to appear at the theatre dressed like a peasant, that would be the grossest and most ridiculous stinginess."[62] Morize has summed up well the mixture of economic and aesthetic considerations in the *Defense du Mondain*: "A certain practical ideal of life, and an economic doctrine; an apology for the epicurean life, frivolous, optimistic, elegant and happy, a sort of hymn to Parisian life, among exquisite things signed by well-known artists, fine dinners, pleasant suppers, and pretty women who are easily won; and on the other hand . . ." his economic theory on the utility of wealth.[63]

Many of the other intellectuals of the time, from Bayle and St. Evremond to Melon, Mandeville, and Montesquieu, had little use for the old frugality.[64] But some of the *philosophes* attacked luxury for its social consequences, for the shallow perspective it revealed concerning the acute problems of social welfare. Diderot especially attacked the luxury of the financiers because it aroused popular discontent and hatred.[65] Garat, later a *conventionnel*, summed up very well the attitude of many of the *philosophes* toward the way of life of the very wealthy: "In the moral code, the bases of which it laid in human nature, philosophy prescribed less austere conduct than did religion; but in the name of happiness, which sensual gratification always promises, and which it gives so rarely, philosophy condemned with the combined appeal of reason, conscience and persuasive ability, those aberrations about which scandals have always been publicized rather than concealed. . . ."[66] And Rousseau, of course, went much further in identifying the luxury and elaborateness of social life with

---

[62] Voltaire, *Dictionnaire philosophique*, III, "Luxe," pp. 923-924 (*Oeuvres complètes*, XXIX-XXXII) (Paris, 1819).

[63] Morize, *L'apologie du luxe*, p. 25.

[64] *Ibid., passim.*

[65] Roustan, *Les philosophes*, p. 185.

[66] Garat, *Mémoires historiques sur le 18e siècle, et sur M. Suard* (Paris, 1821), I, p. 257.

the debasement of social morality and the degradation of social man. It is, after all, perhaps, not so surprising to find the
"emancipated" and victorious bourgeoisie erecting a "Re-
public of Virtue" in 1793. The "old" bourgeois way of life
died very hard, if it died at all; it was rationally and morally
more congruent with the social role of the bourgeoisie in an
open class society than were the efforts of so many of the 18th
century bourgeois to acquire the symbols of noble status.

Of all the bourgeois of the *ancien régime*, none made
greater or, on the whole, more successful efforts to assimilate
to the noble style of life than did the very wealthy Parisian
financiers and a few of the most famous Parisian lawyers,
though even in the provinces there were high-living merchants. These bourgeois had, apparently, no scruples about
social pretension; their attitudes toward luxury were quite different from the hesitant steps toward gracious living that
crept into the way of life of the old bourgeoisie. The old bourgeoisie shared the hostility and contempt of the nobility for
these *nouveaux-riches*, who spent their new wealth in the lavish
manner of the noble class, but often with a lack of aesthetic
discrimination or "taste" that laid them open to ridicule.

All over France, the very wealthiest segment of the bourgeois class was making an undisguised and unabashed bid for
the valued noble style of life. The Mathieu family, mine
owners at Anzin, for example, "are, at bottom, newly en-
riched bourgeois, eager for anything that might distinguish
them, that might indicate publicly their wealth, their drawing nearer to that nobility which they covet."[67] M. Geoffrion,
a member of the commercial elite of the comparatively small
town of Valenciennes, had an annual expenditure of 20,000
livres, which was no more than was expected of such a merchant-manufacturer; Hamoir the Elder, his brother-in-law,
spent 1,000 livres a month on his household alone, and easily
exceeded Geoffrion's annual total.[68] At Montpellier, the style

[67] Rouff, *Les mines de charbon*, p. 223.
[68] Legros, "Les dépenses d'un bourgeois," p. 213.

of life of the wealthiest men of the bourgeoisie was indistinguishable from that of the aristocracy: " 'Ever since finance and commerce have made fortunes quickly for those who have devoted themselves to it, the second order [the bourgeoisie] has gained by its lavish spending and luxury an esteem which the first envies it vainly. By a kind of irresistible process they became mixed. Today, there is no difference between them, in their houses, their food, their dress.' "[69]

The 18th century financiers had almost a craze for building palatial mansions and châteaux, and there was not one of them with whom one or more magnificent residences in Paris or its environs could not be associated. Most of this building occurred between 1730 and 1780, and many of the suburban estates were so fine that they were acquired by the wealthy nobility after the decline of the financiers. Le Bas de Montargis' place at Venves went to no less a noble than Condé, Bernard's at Passy to Boulainvilliers, and Crozat's at Montmorency to the Comte de Luxembourg.[70] Furthermore, besides their interest in building, both the financiers and lesser bourgeois established themselves on these estates for the sake of landownership itself. Ever since the *ordonnance de Blois* in 1579, a *roturier* buying a noble fief could not simply purchase nobility along with it.[71] Except in various outlying provinces which had come late into the monarchy or enjoyed special laws—like Dauphiné, Béarn, and Provence—nobility was *personal* rather than *real*. But even so, and quite apart from the fact that landownership was often a very good financial investment, the bourgeois who aspired to nobility also still felt land to be an essential social investment. Landownership was the supreme symbol of the noble style of life, and ennoblement by other means was felt to be incomplete without it.

[69] Thomas, *Montpellier*, pp. 196-197; Thomas is quoting an acute observer.

[70] Thirion, *La vie privée des financiers*, p. 313.

[71] M. Marion, *Dictionnaire des institutions de la France au 17e et 18e siècle* (Paris, 1923), p. 395.

All over France we find the bourgeoisie buying land: the bourgeoisie of Dijon usually had already acquired such property by the time it entered the Sovereign Courts in the 17th century;[72] the wealthy *armateurs* of Saint-Malo started to buy land from impecunious noblemen, and by the 18th century, the Baude, the Magon, and the Danycan families had spread their possessions all over Brittany.[73] Pichot de la Graverie reported the same phenomenon around Laval,[74] and even J. B. Accarias, a not very wealthy merchant of Die in Dauphiné, felt he had prospered sufficiently by 1706 to buy the small fief of Sérionne and to add its name to his own.[75] The attitude of all these bourgeois landowners is nicely described by Toublet in his account of the life of the successful paper manufacturer, Elie Savatier. By virtue of his manufacturing and mercantile achievements, Savatier had risen to a high position among his fellow-townsmen: "Was it not now admissible for his ambitions to go one step farther, and for him, simple *roturier* that he was, to place himself among the *seigneurs*, who were so proud of their feudal rights? . . . Did not the wealth of our industrialist now permit him to grant himself the luxury of a *château* and the rights that went with it?"[76]

While the greatest degree of luxury is rightly associated with the financiers, it is worth noting that some of the most successful lawyers in Paris lived in the style of great *seigneurs*, as did also many of the younger members of the traditionally more sober *robe*. Eminent lawyers like Gerbier, or Le Normand, whom we have already mentioned, had completely abandoned the sobriety of most of the members of the bar. Le Normand was "a great seigneur of a lawyer, magnificent

---

[72] G. Roupnel, *Les populations de la ville et de la campagne dijonnaise au 17e siècle* (Paris, 1922), p. 187.
[73] Bourde de la Rogerie, *Archives du Finistère*, Série B, III, p. clxix.
[74] Cited in Richard, *Laval*, p. 304.
[75] Accarias, "Jacques Accarias de Sérionne," pp. 495-496.
[76] Abbé E. Toublet, "Un industriel au 18e siècle. Elie Savatier," *Revue historique et archéologique du Maine*, XLVII (1890), p. 93.

in the kind of house he had, the kind of furniture and carriages; he was even more so in his country residence, where he received during the holidays men of high dignity, intellectuals, artists, and his most illustrious colleagues. This style of life, new for a lawyer, made the young members of the bar lose the simple ways of the old."[77] And of Gerbier it is said that he was "sumptuous in his living and worried little about his expenses."[78] At the very top of the professional bourgeoisie, then, the breach with the old ways was sometimes made, but it seemed even less compatible with professional dignity than the luxury of the business elite. Barbier lamented that the abandoning of long black robes by the legal profession detracted from its dignity in the public eye.[79]

Among the wildly extravagant and luxury-loving financiers, there were the classic examples of the absurdly ill-at-ease and miscast *nouveaux riches*, and there were also financiers who easily outdid the nobility in their intellectual and aesthetic sophistication. Manon Phlipon, at the age of eighteen, visited one of the former kind of financiers, the rich son of a *fermier-général*, and she commented that "the caricature of good taste produced here a kind of elegance foreign alike to bourgeois simplicity and to artistic taste. . . . It was worse with the men: the sword of the master of the house, the efforts of the chef . . . could not compensate for the awkwardness of their manners, the deficiencies of language when they wanted to make it seem distinguished, or the commonness of their expressions when they forgot to watch themselves."[80] And there were many others, who were simply rich, spoke badly, and were little read, and who were "the first to laugh at their own ignorance or their solecisms, which, anyway, never kept anyone away from their excellent dinners and their splendid receptions."[81] Beaujon, the court banker, for example, was

[77] Gaudry, *Histoire du barreau*, II, p. 92.

[78] *Ibid.*, II, p. 174.

[79] Barbier, *Journal*, II, p. 346.

[80] Roland, *Mémoires*, p. 97 ff.

[81] Thirion, *La vie privée des financiers*, p. 263.

among those "Turcarets" or "bourgeois gentilshommes," whom, according to Campan, one saw "with a confidence not general with commoners, pronounce impressive words empty of sense, judge without knowing anything about the subject, and brag about their good fortunes."[82] Campan, in fact, preferred the simple, crude, old-style financier to the second generation, which acquired nothing but pride and pretensions and a snobbish contempt for its *roturier* parents.[83]

But more remarkable, perhaps, than the fact that some financiers were uncultivated and pretentious boors, is the large number of these wealthy men who sought to exhibit something more than what Veblen calls "pecuniary ability," who did strive for literary and artistic appreciation, and, in some cases even, performance. They were the new patrons of arts and letters, and as the sponsors of "high-brow" entertainment they also participated in intellectual activities. Grimm wrote that it was ridiculous to accuse these mid-18th century financiers of being mere Turcarets; such men as Caze, de la Porte de Sénancourt, or Grimod Dufort and Lantage de Félicourt were polished men of society.[84] One of these elegant and cultivated financiers was Dupin de Franceuil, one-time lover of Mme. d'Epinay, who taught her much about the world of the salons, both about their rituals and their culture. Helvetius retired from the *fermes* to devote himself to writing, and Lavoisier, the scientist, was an ex-financier. La Popelinière tried his hand at writing, less successfully. Le Normand de Tournehem, La Live de Bellegarde, and Grimod de la Reynière, all collected philosophers and artists around them. Pierre Crozat was a really great art collector, one of a dynasty of Crozats who devotedly and intelligently patronized the arts.[85] His collection of Italian art was really good, and Mariette, one of the greatest art experts of the time, was very much

[82] Campan, *Le mot et la chose* (s.l., 1751), p. 67.
[83] *Ibid.*, p. 65 ff.
[84] Roustan, *Les philosophes*, p. 179 ff.
[85] Thirion, *La vie privée des financiers*, p. 42.

impressed when he catalogued it after Crozat's death in 1743.[86] La Reynière was a genuine lover of music, and gave very enjoyable concerts at his home.[87] Chevrier, too, admitted that these financiers were cultivated men " 'who create the delight of a chosen society, by the pleasures of an elaborate imagination and the charms of a pleasant disposition.' "[88]

By now it must be clearly evident that the bourgeois way of life as a whole, and the differences and changes within it, were closely tied in with the attitudes of the bourgeois toward social mobility. It reflects the conflict between the acceptance of the traditional hereditary class patterning of styles of life, and the desire of the bourgeoisie to rise to the prestigious and esteemed noble pattern of living. More or less, almost all the bourgeois sought the symbols of the noble style of life; more or less they sought to abandon the old bourgeois way of living and to slough off the stigma of their *roture*. The different degrees of change in the way of life of the bourgeoisie are indicative of the conflicts experienced by this class in their quest for mobility. In the next chapter we shall show how these different bourgeois ways of life were related to different patterns and channels of mobility for the bourgeoisie.

[86] A. de Janzé, *Les financiers d'autrefois; fermiers généraux* (Paris, 1886?), p. 62.

[87] *Ibid.*, p. 235.

[88] Quoted in Frederick C. Green, *La peinture des moeurs de la bonne société dans le roman français de 1715 à 1761* (Paris, 1924), pp. 242-243.

# CHAPTER VI

## Changing Patterns of Mobility

THAT the bourgeoisie hoped for and expected a certain amount of upward social mobility is clear from the evidence of the foregoing chapters. Over and over again, the bourgeois revealed in words and in deeds that for all their conservative acceptance of the traditional order of society they nevertheless wished to improve their class position within that order, that their ultimate goal was nobility, and the noble way of life their model. They recognized the superiority of noble status over their own, but, unlike members of a true caste society, they did not accept their position as permanently inferior; rather, they sought, with more or less courage or brashness, to leave behind them everything that stigmatized them as *roturiers*.

By definition, social classes are groups of families who treat each other as equals, and the clearest and final test of such equality is marriage between members of such a group of families. The acid test, therefore, of the successful entry of the mobile bourgeois into a higher social class than that of his parents is his marriage with a member of this higher class. The significance of such a marriage is, presumably, that by virtue of his occupation, his wealth, and his style of life in general, the mobile bourgeois has become the social equal of his marriage partner. There were, in the 18th century, many such marriages between men and women whose parents belonged to different social classes, and though the frequent designation of these marriages as *mésalliances* indicates that they had only limited approval in the society, they are nevertheless proof positive of a considerable amount of social mobility.

Even in our own society, which on the whole tends to play down the importance of class distinctions, the class relations involved in the choice of a marriage partner are the focus of considerable interest or gossip, and they arouse much hope and anxiety. Our egalitarian social values militate against too strong or open disapproval of a "bad" match, but in 18th century France such disapproval was unbridled. In a society which had only limited approval of social mobility, any marriage between members of strikingly different class origins was subject to suspicion if not to condemnation, and these sentiments were generally given full expression. Most liable to such disapproval were, of course, marriages between persons of noble and *roturier* origin respectively, and it was these that were most frequently designated as *mésalliances*.

In one respect, however, the marriage of people of different class origins was institutionally facilitated to a greater degree in 18th century France than in American open class society. The arrangement of marriages *with full provision for a dowry* smoothed the way for the upward marriage of young women, and of men too, belonging to families who had prospered. The dowry was of great importance in marriages between class equals within the *roturier* class, as well as in marriages between children of socially unequal families. In the latter case, especially, the mutual advantage is clear: the dowry was both a social and an economic investment. The Duchesse de Chaulnes put the case neatly and earthily for the financially embarrassed high nobility which was marrying the daughters of the socially ambitious financial elite: "to make an advantageous *mésalliance* is 'to fertilize one's soil,' and God knows the soil needs fertilizing!"[1]

The extent to which wealth did make social mobility possible is shown by the scale of "prices" of husbands in Paris of Louis XIV:

| for a dowry of | 2- 6,000 | you got a | merchant or sergeant |
| " " " " | 12- 20,000 | " " " | notary or registrar |
| " " " " | 20- 30,000 | " " " | solicitor |

[1] Ducros, *La société française*, p. 65.

| for | a | dowry | of | 35- 45,000 | you | got | a | treasurer of France |
|-----|-----|-----|-----|-----|-----|-----|-----|-----|
| " | " | " | " | 45- 75,000 | " | " | " | counselor in the *cour des aides* |
| " | " | " | " | 75-150,000 | " | " | " | counselor in the Parlement |
| " | " | " | " | 200-600,000 | " | " | " | *anyone you wanted.*[2] |

By the 18th century, dowries had risen further. They had always been lower in provincial towns than in Paris, so that it was remarkable when a lawyer's son in Laval now got a dowry of 10,000 livres, and the son of a banker there received as much as 20,000 livres.[3] It is also revealing to trace the increase in the dowries of the daughters of successive generations of a single family, which rose in the 17th and 18th centuries from the petit bourgeoisie to the *robe*. At the beginning of the 17th century, a daughter of the printer Barbou received only 1,000-1,200 livres; by 1647, a girl marrying into the Barbou family had to bring 4,000 livres; and by 1748, Jean III Barbou married his daughter to a small *noble de race*, and gave her 36,000 livres. "They had come a long way since the 1000 livres given to Marie Barbou in 1606, but they readily made a sacrifice for the first gentleman entering the family."[4]

Bourgeois ambitions meshed neatly with noble financial embarrassment, especially in the *grande monde* of Paris, where noble "pride" exerted less pressure than the need to keep up a magnificent way of life, and where the costly symbols of this way of life were so much more important than the ancient and honorable functions attached to nobility. For financial need alone was not in all cases among the 18th century nobility sufficient motivation for a *mésalliance*, i.e., for an admission that the wealthiest bourgeois, at least, must be considered their

[2] Babeau, *Les bourgeois*, p. 249 ff.; these prices are in livres.

[3] Richard, *Laval*, pp. 162-163.

[4] P. Ducourtieux, "Les Barbou, imprimeurs. Lyon—Limoges—Paris. 1524-1893," *Bulletin du Limousin*, XLI (1894), pp. 171-172.

social equals. The poverty-stricken provincial nobility continued to disdain any alliance with the rich bourgeoisie, even though they might be reduced to the status of *hobereaux*. The acceptance by the Court nobility of these marriages may, therefore, be one more indication of its defection from a genuine noble ideology and of its espousal of a way of life no longer congruent with its older functions as a political and military aristocracy. "In Paris, a wealthy *roturière* married a duke and was 'presented' at Court; in the provinces, a *roturier*, however rich he might be, had difficulty marrying the daughter of a ruined marquis."[5] The provincial town of Ponthivy in Brittany seems to have been an exception, however, since daughters of merchants had no apparent difficulty in finding noble husbands. The Métayer family is only one example: they were merchants until 1740, when "they quit commerce, and one of them bought the office of King's counselor. His son married a noble girl of the town."[6]

In Paris there were, indeed, innumerable "fertilizing" marriages, with the result, as Duclos put it, that "the Court and the world of finance were often in mourning for the same person,"[7] and that ". . . the nobility have now lost the right to despise the world of finance, for only few of its members do not have blood ties with the latter."[8] The wealthy financiers of Paris saw their children make marriages of great social brilliance, marriages which involved the greatest names of the old *noblesse* as well as of the *robe*. Here are a few striking examples: Barbier reported in 1752 that "the viscount of Rohan-Chabot has married Mlle. de Vervins, the daughter of a counselor in Parlement, who was the son of M. Bonnevie, a farmer general." The young lady's maternal grandfather had been a cloth merchant on the rue St. Denis.[9] Mme. de la Rouchefoucauld, who bore another name of great distinction,

---

[5] Carré, *La noblesse*, p. 181.    [6] Le Lay, *Ponthivy*, pp. 46-47.

[7] Duclos, *Considérations*, p. 124.

[8] *Ibid.*, p. 125. See also Carré, *La noblesse*, pp. 34-55, for numerous examples of intermarriage.

[9] Barbier, *Journal*, III, pp. 339-340.

was none other than the daughter of "the extremely wealthy Proudre, the tax farmer. . . ."[10] And the same was true of the *robe*. Mlle. de la Reynière, daughter of another farmer general, married the son of Lamoignon de Blancmesnil, and brought over 700,000 livres to the marriage.[11] A Choiseul married the granddaughter of Crozat, a Molé the daughter of Bernard, and the daughter of the banker Laborde became no less than the Comtesse de Noailles.[12] Descazeaux, an old shipowner of Saint-Malo, also did very well with a granddaughter of the Maréchal de Noailles.[13]

Marriage and all the social intimacy attendant upon it should signify the complete social equality of the partners, but the kind of marriages we have described fell somewhat short of such complete equality, and for that reason they were often not successful as marriages. Given the ambivalent class attitudes of the bourgeoisie, which we have already discussed, and the attitudes of the nobility, which we can easily assume to have been equally ambivalent, strains and tensions in such marriages were only to be expected. To be sure, in some cases difficulties may have arisen from the discrepant ways of life of the marriage partners, but such difficulties were undoubtedly enhanced by the unconcealed public disapproval of the marriage and by the mixed feelings of the families immediately involved. In many cases, bourgeois ladies were surely as cultivated as their noble husbands and this may have eased the situation; but it was hard to overcome the strong sentiments against *mésalliances*. The noble husband could escape from the strains of such a marriage into that faithlessness which was, in any case, much more generally accepted among the nobility than among the bourgeoisie. It was the bourgeois wife who felt the failure of the marriage most acutely.

[10] Thirion, *La vie privée des financiers*, p. 58.
[11] Ducros, *La société française*, p. 175.
[12] Lefèbvre, *Coming of the Revolution*, pp. 13-14.
[13] M. Marais, *Journal et mémoires sur la régence et le règne de Louis XV (1715-1737)* (Paris, 1863-1868), I, p. 302.

Barbier commented in 1733 that many people, including himself, disapproved of the marriage of so low-born a woman as the daughter of Bernard to the Marquis de Mirepoix, but he added that she had a dowry of 800,000 livres, and that so much money was not being refused in those days even by a Mirepoix.[14] He was also offended at the excessive splendor of the wedding feast given when Bernard's other daughter married Molé, which surpassed anything customary at princely weddings; and he quoted current *chansons*, "which do no honor to those related by marriage to the Bernard family":

> Oh times, oh manners, oh unruly century!
> When we see our noblest families derogating.
> Lamoignon, Mirepoix, Molé,
> All marry the daughters of Bernard
> And become the receivers of his stolen goods.[15]

In the attitudes of Barbier, who identified, after all, with the sentiments of the nobility, we find reflected the uneasiness the nobleman must have felt at demeaning himself by marrying a *roturière*, and for the girl of the bourgeoisie such a marriage entailed, at best, the fear of "not belonging," and at worst outright humiliation. For example, Crozat's daughter was always referred to in the house of her Bouillon in-laws as "the little ingot of gold";[16] and the marriage of a member of the household of the Prince de Conti to the daughter of the farmer general Haudry, who had a dowry of 400,000 livres, created strange relatives: "this M. Haudry, who arrived by dint of his hard work, has a brother who is a baker in the faubourg St. Antoine, and who has many children. That means to throw oneself in with an uncle and cousins of very

---

[14] Barbier, *Journal*, II, pp. 22-23.
[15] *Ibid.*, II, pp. 36-38:
> O temps, ô moers, ô siècle déreglé!
> Où l'on voit déroger les plus nobles familles
> Lamoignon, Mirepoix, Molé,
> De Bernard epousent les filles,
> Et sont receleurs du bien qu'il a volé.
[16] Marais, *Journal*, II, p. 345.

low rank for a little money."[17] Chevrier, in his *Ridicules du Siècle*, blames the nobility for the failure of so many *mésalliances*, for he thinks they were irresponsibly greedy for wealth alone and abused their bourgeois wives,[18] but the bourgeois fathers, if not the daughters, were actually equally responsible. The deepest cause for the failure of these marriages lay in the *limited* approval of social mobility in French society. This limited approval permitted such a gradual rise through the ranks of the *roturier* class as that of the Barbou, but it was a serious impediment to the dramatic bid the very wealthiest bourgeois made for equality with the high nobility. Below we shall see how this limited approval affected the patterns of mobility, and how its increasing limitation became a threat to the existence of some of these patterns.

French society of the 18th century permitted, then, a certain amount of intermarriage between people whose class origins were different. But how did the mobile individual accomplish his rise in the social scale? What were his opportunities for improving his social class position in such a way that he could eventually "marry up," and even marry into the nobility? In the remainder of this chapter we shall examine the availability of channels of mobility to the bourgeoisie, and especially the *changing* availability of these channels.

The limited approval of social mobility would indicate that channels of mobility were social patterns of only secondary importance, patterns that met with reluctant tolerance from the dominant classes in the society. This was indeed so. The mobile groups benefited from weaknesses in the traditional political and economic structure, from the loss of political and economic power by the old "ruling class," which had little choice but to recognize their new competitors for prestige and authority. The mobile bourgeoisie, to be more specific, had

[17] Barbier, *Journal*, III, p. 120.
[18] Green, *La peinture des moeurs*, pp. 249-250.

wealth and competence, which could be put to good use by the French monarchy in its struggle for power with the feudal nobility. This informal alliance between the monarchy and the bourgeoisie was of great mutual advantage: the monarchy gained the services of capable lawyers and administrators, as well as the financial support of what was fast becoming the wealthiest class in the society; and the bourgeoisie gained the opportunity of making its wealth "respectable" according to the traditional social definition. The bourgeoisie not only bargained for economic privileges—in the form, for example, of town and guild charters—but it also acquired the support of the monarchy against the old nobility in its quest for noble status and the noble way of life.

This acceptance by the bourgeoisie of the traditional definition of social prestige made it possible to integrate the mobile bourgeois into the existing class structure. As we saw in our discussion of the bourgeois's class attitudes, he tended to disparage his own merits; he aimed to have those merits transformed into traditional social virtues. With the backing of royal power, this transformation could be achieved. The bourgeois was enabled to escape his *roturier* status either by direct ennoblement for the purchase of judicial and political offices, or by his admission into such traditionally prestigious occupations as military and ecclesiastical careers. But when the ever-weakening 18th century monarchy was no longer able to back the bourgeois class against the opposition of the nobility, these integrative channels of mobility were increasingly, though never completely, closed off. The non-integrating channels—those depending on the recognition of merit as such, especially intellectual achievement—were not affected by this "feudal reaction."

1. *Venality of Offices.* The venality of offices, and especially of ennobling offices, was the most important of the channels of mobility that enabled the well-to-do bourgeois to dignify his wealth, at the very least by contact with the professional world, and at best by the acquisition of some degree of nobil-

ity. Wealth derived from ignoble, *dérogeant* commercial occupations could be invested in offices, which in many cases
were not remunerative (though as the price of offices rose,
some were excellent financial investments, too) but which always constituted a step upward on the social ladder for the
purchaser. "The venality of offices contributed heavily, in the
France of old, to the upward movement of the inferior classes,
and to the renewal of the ruling classes."[19] It is this positive
function of venality as a channel of social mobility that concerns us here, not the corruption and inefficiency it brought
into the French political and judicial system, which is more
often stressed.[20]

While the leasing of offices goes back to the 14th century, the
office at that time was still considered to be a kind of fief. It
was inalienable in the 14th and 15th centuries; and officeholders were not irremovable, though by the 15th century
there were signs in the direction of hereditary property and
tenure in offices. It was the officials who gradually arrogated
unto themselves the right to treat their offices as alienable
property, and the state came to tolerate this practice, though
until the 17th century it did not confirm the outright ownership of offices.[21] Not until 1604, with the institution of the
*Paulette*, did officials receive far-reaching powers of disposal
over their offices from the state, on condition of an annual
payment of one-sixtieth of the price of the office. The *Paulette*
did not give full rights of inheritance, for the heir had to fill
the office within a year, but it did give greater security than
the purchased *survivance*, which had existed for some time,
but which was revocable.[22] In actuality, the *Paulette* merely
recognized the private ownership of public offices.[23]

---

[19] G. Pagès, "La vénalité des offices dans l'ancienne France," *Revue historique*, CLXIX (1932), p. 492.

[20] M. Goehring, *Geschichte der Grossen Revolution*, Vol. I. *Sturz des
Ancien Régime und Sieg der Revolution* (Tuebingen, 1950), pp. 89-101.

[21] M. Goehring, *Die Aemterkaeuflichkeit im Ancien Régime* (Berlin,
1938), pp. 12-31.

[22] *Ibid.*, pp. 73-76.     [23] *Ibid.*, pp. 84-87.

From the royal standpoint, the venality of offices was one of the most important sources of income, and officeholders were accordingly chosen for their wealth rather than for their competence. The Parlement of Paris claimed as early as 1551, even, that offices were simply sold to the highest bidder.[24] The selling of offices closed the ranks of the *robe* to possible recruits from the lawyer class after the 16th century, since they were easily outbid by the newly eligible merchants. Ford finds two basic patterns in the family backgrounds of *robe* nobility going back to the 16th and 17th centuries: (1) a crossover from big business to the high *robe* in the 16th and 17th centuries, and (2) some business success plus a gradual rise through the official hierarchy, arriving in the high *robe* in the late 17th century.[25] In the Parlement of Aix-en-Provence, for example, many of the magistrates had come from the lawyer class in the 16th century, but with the establishment of venality in the 17th, the adminstration of justice came to be concentrated in the hands of the wealthier merchant group.[26] Throughout the 16th and 17th centuries, when offices were extremely lucrative, huge sums were invested in them by the merchant class. For example, in 1665, the four hundred members of the Parlement of Paris had invested over fifty million livres in their offices.[27]

It was not, however, simply the status of officeholder that the bourgeois coveted when he abandoned commerce for something better. The great desideratum was not merely the attainment of official dignity, but also of nobility, and it was here that wealth really counted. For offices per se were within reach of bourgeois with very little capital; the price range made them available to a wide variety of people. In Poitou, for example, prices ranged from 600 to 35,000 livres: "If the good

[24] *Ibid.*, p. 51 ff.
[25] Franklin Ford, *Robe and Sword, The Regrouping of the French Aristocracy After Louis XIV* (Cambridge, Mass., 1953), p. 128.
[26] Louis Wolff, *Le Parlement de Provence au 18e siècle* (Aix-en-Provence, 1920), p. 17.
[27] Goehring, *Die Aemterkaeuflichkeit*, p. 243 ff.

offices of the provinces were sold dear, an office as President Treasurer of France for 35,000 livres, the lieutenant general-ship of the sénéchaussée of Chatelleraut for 26,000, the criminal lieutenancy of Poitiers for 12,000 livres, on the other hand, the price of the office of notary created at Dissous in 1784 for the son of the postmaster cost no more than 600 livres."[28] But the many available offices entailed, as far as nobility was concerned, anything from no nobility at all to immediate hereditary nobility, and the degree of nobility an office brought was to a large extent correlated with its official dignity and price.

By the 18th century, the highest *robe* offices—those in the Sovereign Courts, both of Paris and most of the provinces that had such courts—conferred hereditary nobility, thanks to the financial embarrassment of the Royal Treasury in the 17th century which made this favor to customers necessary.[29] Other offices ennobling "in the first degree" were those of chancellor, keeper of the seals, secretary of state, counselor of state, master of requests.[30] The offices in the Chamber of Accounts were similarly ennobling, and their price was very high, ranging, in 1771, from the office of first president at 550,000 livres down to the solicitor general at a mere 120,000 livres.[31] For the same price, roughly, one could also buy one of the nine hundred offices of secretary to the king (*sécrétaire du roi*) with first degree nobility. Many offices conferred transmissible nobility if held over a period of years, or if the incumbent died while in office, for example the 1550 offices in the Châtelet.[32] Others became hereditarily ennobling after several generations, such as some of the offices in the financial bureau.[33] Finally, one could acquire offices that entailed personal nobility only. In all, there were, according to an èstimate made by Necker, 4,000 ennobling offices,[34] and Voltaire estimated,

[28] Roux, *La Révolution à Poitiers*, p. 22.
[29] Marcel Marion, *Dictionnaire*, pp. 313-314.
[30] *Ibid.*, p. 393.   [31] *Ibid.*, pp. 81-82.   [32] *Ibid.*, p. 89.
[33] Ford, *Robe and Sword*, p. 54.
[34] Marion, *Dictionnaire*, p. 393.

perhaps conservatively that 10,000 people had been ennobled through officeholding.[35]

If we recall again the crucial importance of upward marriage in the final accomplishment of social mobility, it becomes quite clear why it was *hereditary* nobility that the socially ambitious bourgeois wanted above all to buy, and why the huge sums we quote above were spent on such nobility. But from the 15th century on, offices of all kinds were increasingly sought by the different groups within the bourgeoisie, even those who could not afford an ennobling office. According to Loyseau, 50,000 offices were sold in the second half of the 16th century,[36] and even the owners of small and insignificant offices in some way felt that they shared in the dignity of the whole corps of officeholders.[37] Many of the lower judicial titles sold by the king and *seigneurs justiciers* did not confer nobility, "but they responded to a general need, that of attiring oneself in a robe which brings its wearer a little nearer to the royal magistracy."[38] In Brittany, all the bourgeois who had made some money "hastened to buy one of those innumerable offices which led to nobility, such as those of gentlemen of the grand chase of France, secretary to the king, treasurer of the royal house of France. . . ."[39] Several of those mentioned here were only indirectly ennobling. In the Limousin, too, it was the accepted practice for a family that had become sufficiently wealthy in trade to leave the ranks of the bourgeoisie and enter the *robe*:[40] "Almost all our bourgeois families bought offices which gave them the privileges of nobility. How could the Barbou [a family of printers] not do likewise, after their alliance by marriage

[35] Goehring, *Grosse Revolution*, I, p. 133.

[36] Goehring, *Die Aemterkaeuflichkeit*, p. 291.

[37] *Ibid.*, p. 292.

[38] H. Beaune, "Les avocats d'autrefois," *La Réforme sociale*, 2e série, I (janvier, 1886), p. 15.

[39] Bourde de la Rogerie, *Archives du Finistère*, Série B, III, pp. clxiv-clxv.

[40] Joseph Boulaud, "Livre de raison de Grégoire Bénoist de Lostende (1677-1754)," *Bulletin de la Société archéologique et historique du Limousin*, LIX (1909), p. 93.

with the Flottes, Blondeau, Maillard, . . . whose members were general treasurers of finances?"[41] Buying offices was obviously the 18th century bourgeois' method of "keeping up with the Joneses."

While the middle bourgeoisie could frequently not afford first degree nobility, the very wealthiest bourgeois bought those offices which gave them immediate hereditary nobility. In the 18th century, when, as we shall see presently, many high judicial and political offices were no longer available, the office most frequently bought was that of secretary to the king. The number of these so-called secretaries, who actually held sinecures, varied from 340 in 1704, to 240 in 1724, and again went up to over 300 in 1784. Even in 1784, their price was still as high as 150,000 livres. Before admission to this office, the candidate's profession and that of his family were investigated, and in general only the members of the upper bourgeoisie living in the noble style were considered eligible; those with inacceptable occupations like commerce, who could not get dispensations by *lettres de comptabilité*, had to drop their occupation and wait a few years before they were admitted.[42] Candidates came not only from Paris but also from provincial towns. For example, Jacques Pétiniaud, head of a large banking and importing house in Limoges, decided, at the age of sixty-five, to cap his career by buying this office,[43] and the Alba family of Ponthivy could boast of "Squire Jean Alba, counselor secretary to the king, of the house and crown of France. . . ."[44] Many of the great Parisian financiers acquired their nobility in this fashion: "All those millionnaires who blushed easily at their birth, tried to make themselves re-

[41] Ducourtieux, "Les Barbou," *Bulletin . . . du Limousin*, XLI (1894), pp. 166-167.

[42] Pierre Robin, *La compagnie des secrétaires du roi (1351-1791)* (Paris, 1933), pp. 70-71.

[43] André Demartial, "Achat d'une charge de secrétaire du roi par Jacques Pétiniaud de Beaupeyrat en 1779," *Bulletin de la Société archéologique et historique du Limousin*, LIX (1909), pp. 68-69.

[44] Le Lay, *Ponthivy au 18e siècle*, p. 48.

spectable, either by buying some office which conferred nobility, or by what was called a *Savonnette à vilain* [a soap-ball, presumably for cleaning one's self of one's *roture*]. That is to say, an office as secretary to the king."[45]

Offices in the financial bureaux also were bought by the wealthier bourgeois.[46] One of the most eminent bourgeois of Marseilles, Georges Roux, was honored in 1765 with the high, if honorary, position of counselor of state.[47] His father had become secretary of state of the court of accounts of the province, an office ennobling his descendants if it was held for four generations.[48] In Poitou, those who "were in a position to pretend to nobility" might buy anything from the expensive office of secretary to the king to that of president treasurer of France, which conferred nobility only in the third generation.[49] Mounier of Grenoble, a future member of the Constituent Assembly, bought a royal judgeship for 23,000 livres, a position which carried personal nobility.[50]

This flourishing market in offices in which the bourgeoisie were such active traders became less and less free in the course of the 18th century. As the nobility, both of the sword and of the *robe*, gained power at the expense of the monarchy, the bourgeois found that without royal support it was far more difficult to buy their way into the nobility. The high *robe* was the first of the channels of mobility that closed up against the bourgeoisie. While the lower judicial offices remained readily available, entry into the parlementary *robe* became possible only to those men who were already members of that group by birth. This closing off of the high magistracy can be seen

[45] Pidansat de Mairobert, *L'Observateur Hollandois à Paris*, (*L'Espion Anglois, ou Correspondance Sécrète entre Milord All'Eye et Milord All'Ear*, 1), (London, 1784), p. 260.

[46] Carré, *La noblesse*, p. 9.

[47] Artaud, "Georges Roux," *Revue de Marseilles*, XXXIII (1887), pp. 139-140.

[48] *Ibid.*, XXXII (1886), p. 30.

[49] Roux, *La Révolution à Poitiers*, p. 26.

[50] F. Vermale, "Les années de jeunesse de Mounier (1758-1787)," *Annales historiques de la Révolution française*, XVI (1939), p. 13.

by examining the composition of some of the provincial Parlements. It was the case in Dijon, where "in the 18th century, in effect, all the seats in the Sovereign Courts were occupied by families who were established in these seats as in patrimonial fiefs . . ." and these "fiefs" were now handed on without regard for age or competence,[51] or *even* for wealth. In fact, the sole stipulation was that the new magistrate have four degrees of nobility.[52] In the Parlement of Dauphiné at Grenoble, we find the same phenomenon. Although even in 1756 the social origin of most members could be traced back to bourgeois who acquired *robe* offices as far back as the first half of the 17th century, and only eleven members did not have parlementary ancestors,[53] in 1762 the Parlement formally decreed itself a closed caste: "In order to protect a company so well 'composed' as this one against the intrusion of less pure elements, the edict of May 5, 1762 decided that, henceforth, to be admitted, candidates who do not have magistrates among their direct ancestors must justify their candidacy, with documents, by four degrees of nobility in the paternal line."[54] This, incidentally, helped to create quite a recruitment problem, because many young noblemen simply could not afford to go into the Parlement, whose revenues had been declining steadily,[55] and after the recalling of the Parlement in 1775, the lack of recruits was so acute that the barriers were lowered somewhat.[56] In the Parlement of Provence at Aix we find the same four quarters of nobility requirement put into effect in 1769;[57] and to cite one more case, Sée speaks of the increasing

---

[51] Roupnel, *La ville et la campagne dijonnaise*, p. 180.
[52] Bouchard, *La bourgeoisie bourguignonne*, p. 540.
[53] Jean Egret, *Le Parlement de Dauphiné*, I, pp. 21-22.
[54] *Ibid.*, I, p. 23.
[55] *Ibid.*, I, pp. 28-31.
[56] *Ibid.*, II, pp. 34-35. See the excellent comment by Ford, *Robe and Sword*, pp. 145-146, on the minor significance for such studies as his own, and, we think, the present one, of J. Egret's recent article, "L'aristocratie parlementaire française à la fin de l'ancien régime," *Revue historique*, CCVIII (July-Sept. 1952), pp. 1-15.
[57] Wolff, *Le Parlement de Provence*, p. 19.

formation of a closed caste in the high *robe* at Rennes.[58]

The great d'Aguesseau did not realize that his fine speech, made in 1698, praising the legal profession for its reward of merit and competence, was no longer a very accurate description of the situation even at the time, and would have blown apart the 18th century magistracy: "Those distinctions which are based only on the accident of birth . . . become useless props in a profession in which rectitude alone gives nobility, and in which men are esteemed not for what their fathers have done, but for what they do themselves. . . ."[59] In the 18th century magistracy exactly the contrary held true; far from maintaining d'Aguesseau's principles, the parlementary *robe* "forgot" its *roturier* origins and disdained to admit new members from that class.[60] Only for the very wealthiest financiers was it still possible, in the 18th century, to acquire high *robe* status. Of the sons of Samuel Bernard, one became a parlementary president, and another master of requests (an office that was being preempted also by the high *robe*); Masson de Maisonrouge, son of a farmer general, became president in the court of inquiries; and the sons of Peirenc de Moras and Durey d'Arnoncourt, both farmers general, became masters of requests.[61] But in general it was certainly true that the high *robe* was now a closed caste of parlementary dynasties, families like the Ormesson, Amelot, Trudaine, d'Aguesseau, Machault, Molé, or Chauvelin, whose names, as Capefigue says, are as renowned as Rohan, or Béthune, or Noailles.[62]

As the *robe* closed its ranks, it also spread its tentacles to the administrative hierarchy on the one hand, and to the municipal *cloche* on the other.[63] On the level of local municipal government, to be sure, the prominent bourgeois might

[58] Sée, *Les classes sociales*, p. 148.

[59] Delbèke, *Les avocats au 18e siècle*, p. 164.

[60] Goehring, *Die Aemterkaeuflichkeit*, p. 310.

[61] Carré, *La noblesse*, p. 37; Barbier, *Journal*, IV, pp. 31-32.

[62] J. B. H. R. Capefigue, *Louis XV et la société du 18e siècle* (Bruxelles, 1842), I, pp. 66-67.

[63] Ford, *Robe and Sword*, p. 140 ff.

still attain a small amount of political authority and corre-
sponding dignity. Mercier liked to sneer at the "habitual
fatuity" of men of wealth, which was especially gratified by
the title of alderman.[64] Then as now, too, small offices were
dignified with important sounding titles, and Adrien Delahante, "forester in the first forest of Valois and Nanteuil-le-
Haudoin, called himself pompously counselor of the king."[65]
At Angers, even the wig-makers and the coal-measurers could
use that same title, and, however remotely, catch some of the
king's reflected glory.[66] But even the municipal officeholders
became identified in the 18th century with the parlementary
magistracy, though municipal offices had originated in the free
choice of the citizenry. As the municipal magistracy became
venal and conferred hereditary nobility, the so-called *noblesse
de cloche*, it too became a closed caste, and a new solidarity
developed between the municipal and parlementary magistracy, in spite of their ancient rivalry.[67]

What was true of local government was even more true
of the national bureaucracy. By Louis XVI's reign, almost the
entire administrative personnel was recruited from the *noblesse de robe*. All the intendants, sixty-eight of them, were
now noble, in direct violation of their creator's conception, for
Richelieu had put *roturiers* in the intendancies in the hope
that they would be royal weapons against the nobility.[68] The
noble intendant is a nice symbol of the increasing power of
the nobility, and the fact that it was the *robe* rather than the
*épée* that staffed the intendancies (via the office of *maître de
requêtes*, the most frequent steppingstone to that of intendant)[69] made little difference in an age when the sword and

[64] L. S. Mercier, *Tableau de Paris*, nouvelle édition corrigée et augmentée
(Amsterdam, 1793), II, pp. 22-23.
[65] H. Carré, *La France sous Louis XV* (Paris, 1891), p. 179.
[66] Besnard, *Souvenirs*, I, p. 126.
[67] P. Ardasheff, *L'administration provinciale en France, 1774-1789*
(Paris, 1909), p. 15 ff.
[68] *Ibid.*, p. 24 ff.
[69] *Ibid.*, p. 53.

the *robe* were drawing closer and closer together.[70] Few of the "vile bourgeois" that Saint-Simon complained of so bitterly (though, to be sure, he included even the *robe* in this category), neither Colbert, nor Louvois, could have risen to high governmental office under Louis XIV's successors. For good or ill, the monarch was increasingly surrounded by nobles, both as his ministers and as members of the royal household.[71]

This breach in the old alliance between the monarch and the bourgeoisie, and the consequent exclusion of the bourgeoisie from judicial and political offices, affected the stability of the *ancien régime*. Bouchard observes that the parvenus, cut off from access to honor and authority, lost their attachment to the institutions of the old regime, and that the rigidification of the *robe* was one of the factors in preparing the crisis that meant the collapse of the regime.[72] Pagès sums up rather well the political effect on the bourgeoisie of its deprivation of authority: "France is in the hands of a narrow oligarchy, of bourgeois origin, without doubt, but with interests closely allied to those of the nobility. Is it surprising that the bourgeoisie, which continued to grow wealthy and which was the most enlightened class in the country, but which considered itself dispossessed of its part of public power, is irritated, and that its former loyalty is replaced by disaffection?"[73] The bourgeoisie which expected to find in the acquisition of authority a channel of mobility could well become socially "demoralized" when that expectation was not fulfilled, and we shall see presently that this was not the only area of expectation in which it was to suffer disappointment in consequence of the shift of the balance of power within France.

2. *Letters of Nobility*. Besides the possibility of ennoblement through officeholding, there existed in the *ancien régime*

[70] Ford, *Robe and Sword*, *passim*.
[71] Lefèbvre, *The Coming of the French Revolution*, p. 16.
[72] Bouchard, *La bourgeoisie bourguignonne*, pp. 537-538.
[73] Pagès, "La vénalité," p. 495.

the direct sale of letters patent of nobility by the monarchy. The sale of these letters patent was less of a direct threat to noble functions, and all through the period when access to hereditary nobility was barred to the bourgeoisie by noble opposition, the sale of letters of nobility continued, and made at least personal nobility accessible to the *roturier*. Between 1732 and 1748, there were 1,200 payments for ennoblement by letters patent in Paris alone.[74] As the desirable offices became harder to purchase, the bourgeoisie turned more and more to the letters of nobility to gratify their ambitions, and the purchase of such a letter combined with the acquisition of landed property gave a fair semblance of noble status.

3. *Military Career*. A career as officer in the French army was so closely connected with the life of the nobility as to constitute one of the channels of mobility which integrated the bourgeois into the traditional class structure of the Old Regime. An army commission very rarely conferred actual nobility on the non-noble officer; nevertheless it carried high prestige with it.[75] For over a century before 1781, the *roturiers* were able, with more and less difficulty, to obtain these army commissions, and they became one of those opportunities for mobility which the bourgeoisie expected to be available at least to a limited extent.

The circumstances which made *roturier* careers in the army possible were, not surprisingly, the wealth of the bourgeoisie, and, complementarily, the special need created by the organization and financing of the *ancien régime* armies for officers who *were* men of means.[76] For the officers were to a large extent responsible for the payment and equipment of the troops

[74] Ford, *Robe and Sword*, p. 208.

[75] In sharp contrast to the prestige of the officer was the contempt felt for the common "soldat," who was drawn from the dregs of the population. The militia was generally despised, and almost every bourgeois "who was anybody" succeeded in getting exempted from it. See Albert Duruy, *L'armée royale en 1789* (1888), p. 38 ff.; and Hennet, *Les milices et les troupes provinciales* (Paris, 1884), p. 174.

[76] The Old Regime seems to have been congenitally unable either to take or to leave the bourgeois.

under their command. It was during the wars of Louis XIV that access to the army became fairly easy for the *roturier*. There was considerable "indulgence with regard to the lack of birth of the *roturiers*," because it was so hard to find men of birth with sufficient wealth to fill the positions open.[77] The *roturiers* were eager to meet the need, whereas the provincial nobility could not afford to do so: "In the Nivernais, it was necessary to draw into the *arrière ban* people living nobly. The province had to furnish 40 gentlemen. The intendant soon found 30, 'the majority of whom, he said, will be well equipped, because they are young men living nobly who are not gentlemen, and who will be proud and even happy to serve at the expense of their fathers.' "[78] In 1734, again, the minister of war, d'Armenonvilles, who could not find enough *nobles de race* who wanted to be officers, ordered the intendants to accept the sons of magistrates who lived in the noble style, to whom their parents could give incomes of 1,000 or 1,200, or even as little as 700 or 800 livres.[79]

The direct or indirect venality of army commissions, of course, made the position of the indigent provincial nobleman more difficult still, while it facilitated the "encroachment" of the bourgeoisie. These bourgeois infiltrations into the ancient and honorable profession of army officer occurred in spite of the strong opposition of the nobility, which, however, before the middle of the 18th century at least, had neither the means nor the power to substantiate its objections. As the Comte de Saint-Germain, another minister of war, wrote to Pâris Duverney: " 'In the present state of affairs, it is impossible any longer to accept officers who do not buy their jobs and who cannot provide their own pensions. The whole impoverished nobility which used to make up the strength of the armies is now absolutely excluded.' "[80] The young officer

[77] Louis Tuetey, *Les officiers sous l'ancien régime. Nobles et roturiers* (Paris, 1908), p. 59.

[78] *Ibid.*, p. 10.    [79] Carré, *La noblesse*, p. 157.

[80] Quoted in Léon Mention, *L'armée de l'ancien régime de Louis XIV à la Révolution* (Paris, 1900), pp. 140-141.

had evidently to be self-supporting; he had to be in a position not only to buy a company, but also to be sufficiently independent financially so as not to require a state pension on retirement.[81] Venality in the army was a serious obstacle to the establishment of systematic rules for advancement, but attempts to abolish the evil remained largely ineffective. In 1776, an edict forbade any new venality as being against noble interests,[82] but this did not prevent secret deals, in which the heads of corps accepted as officers the sons of financiers to whom they owed money.[83] While bourgeois wealth did not play as important a part in the army as in the government, still its penetration here was noticeable.[84]

The bourgeois had another qualification, besides wealth, for certain branches of military service, which the nobility lacked. In the artillery, for example, many bourgeois who had relatively small means but considerable education and intelligence could make their superior training count. The nobility had little taste for the necessary studies.[85] Several *roturiers* distinguished themselves as general officers, by virtue of their technical knowledge. The engineer Bourcet and the artillerist Gribeauval were bourgeois with outstanding success, and such famous major generals as Simon Delorme and Favart were ennobled for their services.[86]

Until the middle of the 18th century, the number of *roturiers* who became officers by virtue of their wealth or education was fairly large. At the end of the War of the Austrian Succession there were an estimated 4,000 such officers.[87] There are many scattered references to the presence of *roturiers* in the officer corps. Marais noted in 1721 that a daughter of d'Argenson had married M. Legendre de Collandre, "a major general, the son of the famous Legendre of Rouen,

---

[81] Tuetey, *Les officiers*, p. 129.    [82] Duruy, *L'armée royale*, p. 73.

[83] Carré, *La noblesse*, p. 158.

[84] Albert Babeau, *La vie militaire sous l'ancien régime* (Paris, 1890), II, p. 81.

[85] *Ibid.*, II, p. 88.    [86] Tuetey, *Les officiers*, p. 120 ff.

[87] Babeau, *La vie militaire*, II, p. 82.

one of the greatest *négociants* in the world, all of whose children, who are valiant and highly esteemed, entered military
service and acquired a great reputation in it."[88] Tuetey finds
several *roturier* officers in the Flanders and Roussillon regiments in 1755, and thinks that in the Seven Years' War as
many as one third of the officers were *roturiers*.[89] It has been
estimated that as late as 1789, of 9,500 officers, 1,800 were of
*roturier* origin, and 1,100 had risen from the ranks.[90]

The bourgeoisie found it harder to enter the cavalry than
the infantry, a distinction that probably goes back to the
monopoly by the feudal knights of France of fighting on
horseback. However, the *gendarmerie*, the first cavalry corps
after the Maison du Roi, had been gradually invaded by the
rich bourgeoisie, until, in 1774, out of 1,700 men there were
only 280 noblemen; all other commissions were in the hands
of sons of businessmen, magistrates, or lawyers. The price of
these commissions was very high: a company cost 150,000
livres, a sub-lieutenancy 120,000 livres.[91] This was one of the
few regiments that remained open to the bourgeoisie until
the Revolution.[92]

The sons of the bourgeoisie were eager to advance themselves socially through a military career, even though their
position in the army was far from secure. Often the *roturier*
officer suffered social ostracism and even persecution at the
hands of his noble fellow-officers. He might have considerable
difficulty disciplining officers of inferior rank who were socially superior to him, and he met with unfair practices in the

---

[88] Marais, *Journal*, ii, p. 128.

[89] Tuetey, *Les officiers*, p. 99. Tuetey and Mention seem to include some
of the magistrates as *roturiers*, which we would not do, and which probably
distorts the figures somewhat. The reason for this is, very likely, that even
the *robe* did not seem to *belong* in the army; Ford shows, however, that
in the 18th century the lines between *robe* and *épée* became increasingly
flexible.

[90] Spenser Wilkinson, *The French Army before Napoleon* (Oxford,
1915), p. 101.

[91] Mention, *L'armée de l'ancien régime*, p. 130 ff.

[92] Albert Latreille, *L'armée et la nation à la fin de l'ancien régime, les
derniers ministres de la guerre de la monarchie* (Paris, 1914), p. 187.

advancement of non-noble officers. These difficulties are described in Mauvillon's *Le soldat parvenu*: Mauvillon is full of indignation at the lot of the *roturier* in the army, and he maintains that he got fair treatment only in the artillery.[93] The *roturier* suffered most from the pride of the provincial *hobereaux*, who filled the lower officer ranks, especially in the infantry.[94] In spite of frequent discrimination, however, many bourgeois did make successful careers through the grades up to general officers and became major generals.[95]

In 1750, a law was passed which decreed the ennoblement of all general officers, major generals, and lieutenant generals, and which exempted those lower officers who were *chevaliers de Saint Louis* and had served for thirty years (twenty as captain) from the *taille* for life. The law revived some old edicts ennobling all military officers, which had been permitted to lapse.[96] In the middle of the 18th century, however, the revival of this law was both anomalous and impossible, for it flew in the face of the feudal reaction which was gaining ground, and whose effect on the army we shall discuss. Barbier commented very favorably on the justice of the law, which he felt rewarded military service and made possible tax-free retirement for old soldiers, who would now no longer be in a less advantageous position than petty civil officers.[97] But the law was executed only rarely and capriciously by the ministers of war; it was, indeed, against the "spirit of the times."

As early as 1718, the first of a series of decrees was passed which aimed to bar *roturiers* from officer status. The decree of 1718 required every candidate for a commission, whose father had not been an officer, to present a certificate of nobility, attested by four noblemen; but this decree was not enforced,

---

[93] Green, *La peinture des moeurs*, p. 138 ff.
[94] Tuetey, *Les officiers*, p. 255.
[95] *Ibid.*, pp. 331-332.
[96] *Ibid.*, pp. 260-261.
[97] Barbier, *Journal*, III, 187-188; Babeau maintains that *chevaliers de St. Louis* had *hereditary* tax exemption, but Barbier and Tuetey seem to be more reliable authorities on this point.

and sometimes, moreover, attestation of a noble style of life
was considered sufficient.[98] After 1750, however, the tightening up of anti-*roturier* restrictions by such ministers as Belle-
Isle made it difficult even for princes of the blood to get commissions for their *roturier* favorites.[99] Although in the days of
Louis XIV, there was no limit to a man's advancement, once
he was an officer (he could even become a Marshal of France
with precedence over dukes and peers at Court), in the reign
of Louis XV the nobility was increasingly favored and there
were no more bourgeois marshals like Catinat and Fabert,
until finally under Louis XVI the Ségur law barred all *roturiers* from the officer corps.[100] To help the nobility maintain,
or regain, its hold on the army, the government established
the Ecole Militaire in 1751, which drew three-quarters of its
students from the nobility. Such special education made it possible for the poor nobleman to compete with the bourgeois.[101]
Even in the artillery, which had once been the branch of the
service which particularly welcomed talent, only noblemen
or those living in the noble style were now accepted.[102]

Finally, in 1781, there was passed the famous law exclud-
ing from officer status all who lacked four quarters of nobility,
as attested by the court genealogist. The ordinance did not
entirely close the grades to the *roturier*, for it was not retro-
active, and it did not apply to the artillery or the *chevaliers
de Saint Louis*: it was designed to keep all *roturiers* from becoming sub-lieutenants, except for those who rose through the
ranks.[103] Ségur, the minister of war, whose name the law
bears, was not, according to his son, happy about it: "If the
frauds [false attestations of nobility] we complain of are as
frequent as is supposed, he said, this would only prove the
impossibility of preserving an order of things which everyone

[98] Tuetey, *Les officiers*, pp. 87-89.    [99] *Ibid.*, p. 171.
[100] E. Hocquart de Turtot, *Le tiers état et les privilèges* (Paris, 1907),
p. 54 ff.
[101] Tuetey, *Les officiers*, pp. 37-39.
[102] *Ibid.*, p. 281 ff.
[103] Marion, *Dictionnaire*, pp. 263-264.

wants to evade because it is no longer in harmony with our customs, with the progress in education and wealth of the third estate which is injured by this humiliation."[104] Ségur *père* went on to say that no one could expect the son of a magistrate or wealthy merchant to serve as a common soldier. Ségur *fils* felt, indeed, that this was a measure "which will dispose men favorably toward revolution."[105]

The bourgeoisie did resent, as might be expected, this new "humiliating" restriction of their limited opportunities for social mobility. Even the Marquis de Chérin, a defender of the nobility, had to admit that "It is certain that [this law] is humiliating for the Third Estate."[106] And Mme. Campan, lady-in-waiting to the queen and scarcely a democrat, could see what a blow the law of 1781 was to those bourgeois living in the noble style, when a man "in that class of citizens, justly respected, an individual, long employed in diplomacy, having even been honored with the title of minister plenipotentiary, kin of colonels, and on his mother's side, nephew of a lieutenant general with the *cordon rouge*, [could not] have his own son accepted as sublieutenant in an infantry regiment."[107] This was obviously a terrible slap at the mobile bourgeois whose apparently sucessful entry into the noble circles was now being questioned. "While the interests of the bourgeoisie were seriously hurt, it resented above all the wound to its pride."[108] The clause in the law favorable to the sons of *chevalier de Saint Louis*, who came for the most part from the ranks, and therefore from the "people,"[109] must only have made the pill more bitter for the bourgeois to swallow.

[104] Louis Philippe, Comte de Ségur, *Mémoires, souvenirs et anecdotes* (F. M. Barrière, ed., *Bibliothèque des mémoires relatifs à l'histoire de France pendant le 18e siècle*, XIX, XX) (Paris, 1890), I, p. 159.

[105] *Ibid.*, I, p. 277.

[106] L.-N.-H. Chérin, *La Noblesse considérée sous divers rapports, dans les assemblées générales et particulières de la nation* (Paris, 1788), p. 161.

[107] Mme. Campan, *Mémoires sur la vie de Marie-Antoinette. . . .* (F. M. Barrière, ed., *Bibliothèque des mémoires relatifs à l'histoire de France pendant le 18e siècle*, X) (Paris, 1849), p. 179.

[108] Tuetey, *Les officiers*, p. 197.      [109] *Ibid.*, p. 192.

It is not easy to estimate the effectiveness of the Ségur law. The consensus among authorities seems to be, though, that the number of new *roturier* officers was at least very severely limited. Tuetey maintains that of the 2,943 places that became vacant in the infantry and cavalry between 1781 and 1789, all were filled by noblemen with four quarterings,[110] and Hocquart de Turtot thinks that if any non-nobles were promoted at all after 1781, they had attained officer rank before that.[111] Duruy gives some useful statistics: "In 1789, out of 11 marshals, I find 5 dukes, 4 marquis, 1 prince and 1 count; out of 193 lieutenant-generals, all are noble, only nine were untitled; out of 770 major-generals, only 136 were untitled, and 46 had no particle, which does not necessarily mean that they were not noble. Out of 113 infantry brigadiers, 39 only were not titled, and 8 had no particle. . . . So much for the general officers. In the lower grades, among the colonels, one finds the same exclusively aristocratic composition: 9 princes, 5 dukes, 25 marquis, 40 counts, 12 viscounts, 7 barons, 5 knights, 6 untitled, for 109 infantry regiments."[112]

These statistics suggest that the policy of exclusion had considerable success. Only Kolabinska claims that the pressure of the bourgeoisie for mobility through the army was too great to be blocked by the law of 1781, and that in 1787, out of around 2,400 students in the military schools, there were still 800 *roturiers*.[113] Be that as it may, the bourgeois in the latter half of the 18th century might well feel aggrieved about his treatment by the army,[114] and he must have felt that the increasingly limited approval of his social goals put a strain on his loyalties. The army constituted one more channel of mobil-

[110] *Ibid.*, p. 219.
[111] Hocquart de Turtot, *Le tiers état*, p. 57.
[112] Duruy, *L'armée royale*, p. 83.
[113] M. Kolabinska, *La circulation des élites en France. Etude historique depuis la fin du 11e siècle jusqu'à la Grande Révolution* (Lausanne, 1912), pp. 91-92.
[114] There is occasional expression of such resentment in the *cahiers*; see Tuetey, *Les officiers*, p. 218.

ity that had formerly been available to him and which was now being at least partially closed.

4. *Ecclesiastical Career*. The history of bourgeois mobility through an ecclesiastical career is, if not exactly parallel to that of the army, somewhat similar. The break in the Church between the *roturier* lower clergy and noble upper clergy was almost as sharp as that in the army between the *soldat* and the officer, though the parish priest did receive more respect in the *lay* world. In the clergy, there was even much less possibility of rising through the ranks than in the army.

With some local variation, the lower clergy was, by and large, recruited from the bourgeoisie or from the peasantry.[115] Groethuysen exaggerates when he says that the lower clergy was entirely "du peuple" and that no good bourgeois was ever to be found in the priesthood.[116] This might be true of the clergy in village parishes, who were drawn from the petit bourgeoisie of the towns and from the peasantry;[117] but the members of the cathedral chapters of medium importance, of the collegiates and of urban parishes, were to a large extent bourgeois.[118] In the diocese of Arras, and in northern France more generally, several years of higher education were required for ordination, that is, four or five years in the seminaries of Douai or Tournai,[119] and such a requirement for professional training could be met only by bourgeois of some means. In Poitou, even the sons of noblemen entered the lower clergy, but this is atypical.[120]

Though the lower clergy was very poorly paid, yet it was an attractive career to the young bourgeois. It provided a certain security, there were opportunities for education, and even the lower clergy had some share in the dignity of the First

[115] Roustan, *Les philosophes*, p. 307.

[116] Groethuysen, *L'esprit bourgeois*, p. 43.

[117] P. de la Gorce, *Histoire réligieuse de la Révolution* (Paris, 1917), I, p. 23.

[118] *Ibid.*, I, pp. 51-52.

[119] Maurice Braure, *Lille et la Flandre wallonne au 18e siècle* (Lille, 1932), p. 634.

[120] Roux, *La Révolution à Poitiers*, p. 23.

Estate. Young bourgeois who entered the badly paid clergy were similar to those who entered the overcrowded legal profession in order to escape the stigma of commerce and to be associated however remotely with the prestige of the *robe*. Young Besnard was destined by his parents for the priesthood, because they "envisaged [this occupation] . . . according to the accepted opinion of the times, as uniting all desirable advantages, both for him who entered it, as well as for the other children, to whom his inheritance naturally reverted."[121] For many young bourgeois, like Morellet, for instance, entering the priesthood was a good way to obtain an education, for the Jesuits were eager to give the more intelligent among their elementary students further training.

The enormous gulf that existed between the upper clergy and the lower was created not so much by the alleged skepticism of the former and the piety of the later, but by the class difference between them, which was even harder to bridge than in the army. There were fine bishops, like Boisgelin at Aix, Conin de St. Luc at Quimper, and La Rochefoucauld at Beauvais, and there were many members of the lower clergy who were indifferent to religion. However, ". . . basically, the discord between them was caused, above all by the difference in origins, in status . . . in preoccupations, in state of mind." As Sicard says, "What an abyss between a Rohan, who has a resounding name, and a million to spend, and a poor *congruiste*."[122] The common calling which might have united the whole clergy could not overcome class barriers of this kind; instead, strong political ties developed between the lower clergy and the "peuple," or the Third Estate as a whole.

As in the army, high ecclesiastical offices became, in the course of the 18th century, increasingly reserved for members of the nobility, and for a bourgeois the lower clergy was "the end of the line" as far as social mobility was concerned. This,

---

[121] Besnard, *Souvenirs*, I, pp. 1-2.

[122] Abbé Sicard, *L'ancien clergé de France* (Paris, 1905), I, pp. 338-339; the *congruiste* was dependent on a fixed salary.

in turn, only broadened the gulf between upper and lower clergy, and indicated clearly that there were two, not three, Estates in France. Under Louis XIV, *roturiers* could attain high ecclesiastical dignity, though the most important bishoprics were apparently set aside for the high nobility. Thus, Bossuet could not become bishop of either Lyons or Paris, in spite of his genius and reputation. But there were many *roturier* bishops, like Ancelin of Tulle, Sarguin of Senlis, or Dacquin of Fréjus, to mention only a few.[123] In the 18th century, the appointment or promotion of a bourgeois to a bishopric became rare, and though the nature of the priesthood did not permit legislation against such promotions, in effect the same rule was applied as in the army. The parish priest had little or no hope of advancement. "Except in three or four 'lackey's bishoprics,' there were no such positions for anyone without [noble] ancestors."[124] Though the episcopate could not be called a caste, since it was not self-recruited, it became increasingly the exclusive prerogative of the nobility: "It is true, that [even] in 1750 there were only noble Cardinals; but the *Almanach Royal* contains the names of about ten *roturier* prelates, which is still an appreciable number; . . . . Under Louis XVI, a greedy nobility succeeded in claiming all the important positions in the Church as well as in the State as its monopoly. . . ."[125] Out of one hundred and thirty-five bishops, there were still about twenty *roturier* in 1740, but in 1783, at the death of the bishop of Senez, there was not a single *évêché de laquais* left.[126]

The ambitious bourgeois could easily see that by this time the possibilities for mobility in an ecclesiastical career were definitely limited. In Poitou, where the restrictions against non-nobles were perhaps less rigid than elsewhere, the sons of merchants could become members of the cathedral chapter

[123] *Ibid.*, I, pp. 4-5.
[124] Chérel, *De Télémaque à Candide* (Paris, 1933), p. 76.
[125] L. Dollot, *La question des privilèges dans la seconde moitié du 18e siècle* (Paris, 1941), p. 14.
[126] *Ibid.*, p. 51.

of St. Hilaire, and this chapter defended itself in 1790 by claiming that it had never demanded proofs of nobility.[127] Some cathedral chapters were much less easily accessible, with Strassburg, Lyon, and Marseilles, for example, entirely closed to non-nobles.[128] Again in Poitou, "The functions of vicar general, and some royal abbeys, were granted to priests of modest birth. Prejudice closed only the episcopacy to them, *but it closed it absolutely at the end of the 18th century. . . .*"[129] More generally, *roturiers* could still become vicar generals in the 18th century (a kind of administrative assistant to the bishop), but among the vicar generals only the noblemen were further selected for bishoprics. And though the *roturier* vicar generals did very good (and dirty) work, they were never really accepted at the bishop's "court"; they were relegated "to the end of the table, part friends, part servants."[130] "The discontent of the lower clergy became understandable; all that the priests and vicars, generally well educated and from the good bourgeoisie, could expect, at the very best was a canonicate."[131]

Ecclesiastical offices were an excellent method the monarchy had of compensating the nobility for its loss of political power,[132] and also of giving something more respectable than outright pensions to demanding and impecunious nobles. This latter aim was fulfilled especially successfully by the institution of the "sleeping abbot" (*abbé commandataire*), who had no priestly functions whatever.[133] The total number of these benefices at the king's disposal was very large; in all, the king could distribute 20,000 benefices *without care of souls*,[134] and

---

[127] Roux, *La Révolution à Poitiers*, p. 24.

[128] Marion, *Dictionnaire*, p. 97.

[129] Roux, *La Révolution à Poitiers*, p. 25; our italics.

[130] Sicard, *L'ancien clergé*, I, pp. 289-290.

[131] Dollot, *La question des privilèges*, p. 52.

[132] Martin Goehring, *Weg und Sieg der modernen Staatsidee in Frankreich vom Mittelalter zu 1789* (Tuebingen, 1946), p. 10.

[133] Hocquart de Turtot, *Le tiers état*, p. 59.

[134] D. Desdevizes du Dezert, "L'église et l'état en France depuis l'édit de Nantes jusqu'à nos jours. L'église au 18e siècle," *Revue des cours et con-*

pressure from the nobility made it impossible for the king to permit the bourgeoisie to share in the good things of the Church.

So, while the lower clergy still provided limited opportunities of social mobility for the small bourgeois, those *roturiers* with great talent and higher ambitions, like Bossuet in the 17th century, could no longer have successful careers in the Church. With no *évêchés de laquais* left in 1789, it is not surprising that the lower clergy identified itself with the revolutionary forces,[135] or that "the seizure by the nobility of the episcopacy and the best benefices aroused vehement protests in 1789."[136] The ambitious bourgeois might well feel particularly wronged by the establishment of a caste monopoly in the Church, where, above all, virtue should have been rewarded.[137] The rigidification against social mobility in the Church particularly put a strain on the bourgeois *curé*, torn as he was between Christian universalist values (and his stake in these) and traditional Catholic reverence for authority and for tradition itself. This conflict, which members of the Church-in-the-World have had to face since the beginning, at the end of the 18th century tied in with the more widespread ambivalence on this score in French society, and added fuel to the flame of social revolution.

5. *The Noble Style of Life.* Last among those channels of mobility by which the bourgeois sought to become integral members of the traditional class structure is adoption of the noble style of life. In Chapter V we discussed the variations in the bourgeois style of life, including their attempts at *vivre noblement*, with the aim of showing how these ways of life reflect the class attitudes of the bourgeoisie, and especially the conflicts in those attitudes. Here it is worth recalling

---

*férences*, XIV[2] (1906), p. 214; de Turtot's figures are somewhat different, but the net impression is the same, that of a large number of these sinecures.

[135] Dollot, *La question des privilèges, passim.*
[136] Sicard, *L'ancien clergé*, I, pp. 30-31.
[137] *Ibid.*, p. 32.

the different efforts made by the bourgeois to assimilate to the noble way of life, in order to point out that the status symbols involved could be actively manipulated in the interest of social mobility. There is considerable evidence to show that, though the bourgeois always ran certain risks of disapproval and ridicule when he lived like a nobleman (when he built fine mansions, dressed elaborately, and patronized the arts), nevertheless this style of life did often pay off in acceptance on terms of equality by the nobility. When it came to accepting non-noble officers into the army because of the lack of sufficient well-to-do noble ones, for example, the intendants chose these *roturier* officers from among those who at least lived nobly. In marriages between the daughters of financiers and the sons of the nobility it was of great importance that husband and wife "take the same things for granted," and, indeed, many noble husbands were delighted with the wit and cultivation of their bourgeois wives.[138] The active manipulation of the symbols of noble living was a necessary part of the attempts made by some bourgeois to avail themselves of those channels of mobility which integrated the mobile individual into the traditionally prestigious nobility.

6. *Intellectual Achievement and Education.* Of all the mobile *roturiers*, only the intellectuals and artists claimed respect on their own merits. The career of the intellectual, unlike that of the soldier or priest, was esteemed not so much because it was traditionally sanctified as conferring prestige, or because it was ennobling, as was that of the magistrate, but because the men of letters had come to fulfill a function that was felt to be of great importance. This esteem for intellectual achievement opened a channel of mobility to talented men which did not confine them to those activities which were closely associated with the noble style of life. They gained respect because they fulfilled a social need that had, perhaps, not been felt so acutely since the intellectual upheaval of the Renais-

[138] Ducros, *La société française*, p. 176.

sance period: a need for the clarification and reinterpretation of social values, and for concrete commentary on "social problems."

Just as the professional soldier gains in respect and importance in time of war, so also did the professional intellectual gain in stature at a time when social morality was in a state of change and confusion. The traditional religious-aristocratic *Weltanschauung* was threatened by the new rationalistic outlook, of which the intellectuals were partly the creators and partly the interpreters. The fact that has so often been stressed in historical literature, that the 18th century men of letters communicated so well and so easily with the educated lay public, is perhaps just another indication of the real need for "enlightenment" on the part of that public. The charge is often made that 18th century literature is not great art, or at least that it is prosaic, didactic art, and this too shows that the men of letters of the 18th century were called upon to teach and enlighten as well as to entertain. And unlike many of the intellectuals of earlier centuries, the primary emphasis of the thinkers of the Enlightenment was on *secular* matters; in earlier times, the intellectual in his role as preacher and sermonist was ultimately concerned with salvation.

The participants in the salons for which the French intellectual scene of the 18th century is so famous had more than the usual frivolous interest in these gatherings; they had, too, a very serious concern for social, economic, and political problems.[139] And for those who congregated in the salons, the leading intellectuals of the time had become "the respected guides of the nation's thought to whom they listened carefully."[140] The noble and the bourgeois, who were both confused in different ways about their proper place in society, about economic inequality or the desirability of "good" government, came to the salons for more than intellectual stimulation:

[139] Roger Picard, *Les salons littéraires et la société française (1610-1789)*, (New York, 1943), pp. 138-139.
[140] Gaiffe, *Etude sur le drame*, p. 80.

"The fashion, the taste for intellectual pleasures, are insufficient to explain the privileged treatment the men of letters received. In that uneasy world, that had ceased to believe in its own stability, the men of letters had little by little changed into philosophers, who were deeply concerned with the public welfare, and they became moral leaders. . . . Henceforth people expected more from writers than entertainment: they expected to have some insight into the future course of events."[141] Wit was *de rigueur*, to be sure, but it had to be socially significant wit; it had to play on the immediate social problems of France, and, perhaps, soften their harsh reality with humor. The type of "universal" generalization (based on "natural" law) that was so popular always had relevance to some current problem, whether it concerned religion, political organization, or the nature of man.

A great many of the intellectual celebrities of the time were men who rose from very humble family origins to positions in which they dealt on terms of considerable intimacy with the social elite. Marmontel was a "fils du peuple" from Bort in the Limousin whose inclinations drew him to the college at Clermont and thence to Paris, where he became a respectable second rate intellectual, instead of becoming a small town merchant as his father had planned.[142] Diderot's father was a cutlery maker at Langres, Sedaine's a bricklayer, and Rousseau's, of course, a watchmaker. Beaumarchais was another watchmaker's son, and Voltaire could claim no more than a notary for a father. The careers of these men, as Taine stresses, represent a real triumph of talent.[143]

The intellectuals of 18th century French society received a degree of social recognition and esteem from the nobility which was surprising and impressive to a sophisticated visiting Englishman like Arthur Young. He commented that: "The society

[141] Glotz, *Salons*, pp. 21-22.
[142] Mornet, *Les origines intellectuelles*, p. 189 ff.
[143] Taine, *L'ancien régime*, p. 409.

[in France] for a man of letters, or who has any scientific pursuit, cannot be exceeded. The intercourse between such men and the great, which if not upon an equal footing, ought never to exist at all, is respectable. Persons of the highest rank pay an attention to science and literature and emulate the character they confer."[144] In London, it was not so, says Young; there, a Fellow of the Royal Society, for example, would not be received in a "brilliant circle." Gibbon, too, who made his first visit to Paris in 1763, gives suggestive testimony to the interest his French hosts seemed to have in the man of letters rather than in the man of gentle birth. Referring to the very favorable reception of his *Essay* there, he wrote: "This reputation nevertheless caused me one small dissatisfaction. It resulted in my being regarded solely as a man of letters. That quality may be in itself the first in society, but I should have liked to add to it that of a man of rank for which I have such indisputable claims. I did not want the writer to eclipse the gentleman entirely."[145] A certain measure of real equality and mutual respect existed between Parisian bourgeois and nobles who shared intellectual interests and cultural pursuits; in this segment of their lives, class origins were partly forgotten. The lavish entertainments of the farmers general had the function of promoting a rapprochement of classes and of providing a kind of "neutral ground" where people of high birth and great talent might meet.[146]

There were, however, limits, however vaguely defined, to the degree of equality and intimacy with which the bourgeois intellectual could treat his noble friends. The most striking evidence of the existence of a barrier is the absence of marriages between the children of the nobility and of the intellectuals—the only such marriage that comes to mind is that

---

[144] Young, *Travels*, p. 104.

[145] Cited in D. M. Low, *Edward Gibbon, 1737-1794* (London, 1937), p. 130.

[146] De Janzé, *Financiers d'autrefois*, p. 302; see also Ducros, *La société française*, p. 353.

of Diderot's daughter with M. de Vendeul.[147] As spokesmen of a powerful new group, the bourgeois intellectuals were treated with a mixture of awed respect and condescension. This ambivalence is reflected in the position of the intellectuals in the salons, where they were at once the tools of socially ambitious *roturiers* like Mme. Geoffrin or the financiers, or of intellectually ambitious noblemen, like the Prince de Conti, and the masters of these same hosts and hostesses. And it comes out even more clearly in the frequently strained relations between the intellectuals and their *seigneur* patrons.

The social composition and the "atmosphere" of the different salons varied considerably, though this variation does not appear to depend to any great extent on the social origin of its literary celebrities, but rather on the social status of its host or hostess. At the Prince de Conti's were found "the people of very high society, which were also to be found at the marquise du Deffand's."[148] The Prince de Conti invited chiefly men and women of high birth, but this did not mean that Rousseau could not leave the circle of Mme. d'Epinay, a "milieu de finance," for that of the Prince,[149] and could thenceforth count the same Prince, as well as the Duke of Luxembourg, among his friends and protectors.[150]

In addition to the salons of these nobles, other very successful salons were conducted by many bourgeois. "Mlle. de Lespinasse was . . . nothing more than an 'adventurer,' Mme. Geoffrin was only a petite bourgeoise, and Mme. Necker had more money than nobility."[151] The success of Mme. Geoffrin's salon may have been, in part, connected with its very bourgeois-ness: "There one received a warm and comfortable

---

[147] The Vendeul family has only recently permitted access to the Diderot papers—evidence that they were a good deal less than proud of their connection with the prominent *philosophe*.

[148] Glotz, *Salons*, p. 157.

[149] *Ibid.*, p. 157.

[150] Barbier, *Journal*, IV, p. 437.

[151] Daniel Mornet, "La vie mondaine, les salons," *La vie parisienne au 18e siècle*. Leçons faites à l'école des hautes études sociales (Paris, 1914), p. 140.

welcome, without being overwhelmed by princely splendor or the slightly too gaudy luxury of the financier. There one felt none of those constraints, which, in spite of everything, embarrassed the guests in the great aristocratic salons."[152] This quality of Mme. Geoffrin's salon appealed especially to foreign visitors. The showy luxury of the financiers did not, however, keep the very "best" and more interesting people away from their gatherings. La Popelinière counted among his guests the Maréchal de Richelieu, the Maréchal de Saxe, the duc d'Aiguillon, *gens de lettres* like Voltaire, Buffon, and Diderot, adventurers like Casanova, and artists like Van Loo.[153] Mme. Vigée Lebrun recollected with pleasure that she met, at La Reynière's, the comtesse de Ségur, the abbé Barthelémy, and others; she felt that years later it was impossible to recapture or understand the wit and elegance of those gatherings.[154]

In all these salons, the laity, whether of the nobility or of finance, came away with new ideas and insights, with some degree of enlightenment. And the intellectuals, for their part, acquired a certain urbanity and politeness, and learned to communicate their ideas in clear and palatable form. The egalitarian spirit, and the mutual benefit that the intellectuals and their public derived from the meetings, should not be underestimated. Although the different mistresses of the salons exercised a certain amount of censorship over the subjects of discussion, the discussions were carried on as among equals, with the intellectual in the seat of honor. One of the things that soured Voltaire on his position at Potsdam was just this fact: that there he was only part of Frederick's court, and not the central attraction.[155] In the "society of free spirits which was composed of the great men of intellect, of birth or of

[152] Picard, *Les salons*, p. 214.
[153] *Ibid.*, pp. 295-296.
[154] Quoted in Gustave Desnoiresterre, *Grimod de la Reynière et son groupe* (Paris, 1877), pp. 19-20.
[155] Glotz, *Salons*, pp. 11-12.

wealth,"[156] the current social distinctions could not be completely abandoned (dukes were always given their full titles), but still, it was a society drawn together by mutual interests rather than by class equality, in which men lost themselves in these interests at least for the duration of the meetings and partly forgot the social distinctions that separated them.[157]

This was true not only in the salons of Paris, but also in many of the provincial academies.[158] It does not, however, seem to have been the case in Bordeaux, the home of Montesquieu, and the difference is striking: "Bordeaux society did not afford . . . these rapprochements [between nobility and talent]. In effect, the same men represented at the same time the nobility, and arts and sciences. . . . It was in the Parlement that the town of Bordeaux recruited, in the 18th century, her nobles and her intellectuals."[159] In Dijon, too, the Academy, after a "democratic" beginning, became more and more exclusively *robe*.[160] This kind of exclusive monopoly of intellectual activities by one class was, on the whole, the exception rather than the rule.

The fact that the intellectual world *is*, at bottom, universalistic in its values is most clearly evident in the constitution and principles of the Académie Française. These principles were never violated in all its history up to the Revolution. "The essential principle on which Cardinal Richelieu had founded the Academy was equality. There was to be among the academicians neither the distinction nor the advantage given by birth, rank or dignities; no difference in the treatment they received from each other; no privilege for rank. . . ."[161] These principles were not violated even when, in the reign of Louis XV, the comte de Clermont, a prince of the

[156] Picard, *Les salons*, p. 149.

[157] *Ibid.*, p. 148 ff.

[158] Mornet, *Les origines intellectuelles*, p. 151.

[159] Théodore Froment, "Un salon parlementaire à Bordeau au 18e siècle," *Revue philomatique de Bordeaux et du Sud-Ouest*, I (1897), p. 114.

[160] Bouchard, *La bourgeoisie bourguignonne*, *passim*.

[161] F. Masson, *L'Académie Française, 1629-1793* (Paris, 1912), p. 11.

blood, was elected; this election, for all its potential danger to academic equality, served only to confirm it, since the prince received no different treatment in the Académie than anyone else.[162]

Outside the Académie, intellectual achievement could not hope to meet with such unqualified respect. Many of the greatest writers had stormy relations with their noble friends, although they also received flattering admiration and material aid. But, ". . . on both sides, it was never felt that one had sufficient respect for the other."[163] The relations of Voltaire and Rousseau with their friends "du grand monde" show an alternation of conflict and differences, on the one hand, and "enthusiasms" on the other, the former being caused by the forgetting of social distances by the intellectuals and by hurtful disdain on the part of the nobility.[164] Even Voltaire could not afford to forget a certain respectful attitude toward his noble friends and acquaintances. Collé may not have exaggerated when he said: " 'There are noblemen who are capable of friendship, but men of letters should expect it only from their equals.' "[165] For all the kindness shown by the wealthy *seigneurs* to the writers, there was sufficient *amour propre* involved to cause trouble, and even in the case of bourgeois patronage of arts and letters, the dependent status of the artist brought a certain amount of friction. Rousseau was neurotically sensitive about his social "inadequacy" and his social humiliations, but his was only the most extreme form of a common discomfort, a common insecurity. The fact that patronage was now problematic sheds light from a new angle on the larger problem of the limited approval of social mobility in French society. It made it impossible for men of genius in literature and art either to win full acceptance and recognition of their competence from men of noble families or to be content to be their dependents.

[162] *Ibid.*, p. 197.  [163] Carré, *La noblesse*, p. 212.
[164] *Ibid.*, p. 213.  [165] Quoted in Carré, *La noblesse*, p. 223.

Tangentially to the question of the mobility of the intellectual, that is, the man of superior education and talent with a dedication to working with ideas, we shall discuss briefly the orientation of the bourgeois toward education in general. The bourgeois "believed" in education; it was congruent with the existence of a rational compartment in his values that he should be a precursor of the 19th century liberal in his faith in education. The bourgeois had great respect for education, and if he could afford it, he availed himself of the educational opportunities. The enrollment in the colleges was mostly recruited from the bourgeoisie.[166] In Tulle, for example, the bourgeois would send his children to the local college if it was financially possible.[167] In Caen, the upper bourgeoisie was far more concerned than the nobility with the matter of good education, and bourgeois fathers supervised their children with great solicitude.[168] J. J. Mounier was sent to the Collège Royale-Dauphin at Grenoble at the age of twelve; this decision indicated that the affairs of his shopkeeper father had prospered, and that his parents hoped to give their oldest son the kind of liberal education that would enable him to mingle with the nobility and upper bourgeoisie of Grenoble.[169] The collège of Anjou, which Larévelliere-Lépeaux attended, theoretically accepted students from all social classes, "the majority of pupils, however, came from non-noble but well-to-do families."[170]

Money spent on education was considered to be well spent, for the bourgeois realized that his superior competence depended very largely on it.[171] The success of the bourgeois artillery officers is a case in point. Again, the young Duclos at Dangeau's school in Paris recalled that "I felt very soon

[166] Ducros, *La société française*, p. 202.
[167] Fage, *La vie à Tulle*, pp. 78-79.
[168] Vanel, *La vie publique à Caen*, p. 41.
[169] Vermale, "Jeunesse de Mounier," p. 4.
[170] Georgia Robison, *Revellière-Lépeaux, Citizen-Director, 1753-1824* (New York, 1938), pp. 25-26.
[171] Ducros, *La société française*, p. 286.

that I could only distinguish myself from the little counts and marquis by some superiority in other regards," and that the little bourgeois boy who was a good student did "enjoy obvious respect on the part of his comrades."[172] At the Collège Louis-le-Grand in Paris, the students were rewarded on the basis of merit as far as their studies were concerned, although class differences did affect their styles of life: "All the students were treated by the Fathers on an equal footing. The best ones had the title of academicians, and noble or otherwise, preceded all the others. However, the sons of great noblemen had rooms and a valet for their service . . . The others lived 15 or 20 in a room, under the supervision of a *cubiculaire*."[173] Scholastic achievement could play some part, at least, in overcoming the social handicap of *roturier* birth, and the mobility-conscious bourgeoisie was not likely to overlook its possibilities.

Eighteenth century French society, then, gave limited approval to social mobility, and provided, correspondingly, limited opportunities for the achievement of such mobility. It was the bourgeoisie that benefited most from these opportunities, for it had the wealth and competence which were the prerequisites of social improvement. The bourgeoisie could afford the price of "disembarrassing" itself of its despised way of life and of assimilating to the esteemed noble style. And so long as the monarchy had the power to do so, it made available to the bourgeoisie noble status and its symbols—at a price. As the balance of power shifted to the nobility, however, it became increasingly possible for the nobility to bar the bourgeois from access to its ranks, and the available channels of mobility were even more limited. The old honorable functions, such as judicial, political, and military office, were closing, and it became more difficult for the mobile individual to become integrated into the traditional aristocratic

---

[172] Duclos, *Mémoires*, pp. 10-11.
[173] Desdevises du Dezert, "L'église et l'état," p. 217.

class structure. This rigidification of the class structure of 18th century France had potentially far-reaching consequences, in view of the already divided moral allegiance of the class most affected by it, the bourgeoisie, and it is these wider implications that we shall discuss in our concluding chapter.

# CHAPTER VII

## Conclusion: The Position
## of the Bourgeoisie in the Class Structure
## and the French Revolution

IN the society of 18th century France, in which men fell into two broad groups, that of noble and that of non-noble or *roturier* origin, the non-noble bourgeoisie was in a peculiar position. More than any other group, the bourgeoisie was affected by the fact that this was a society which gave limited approval to social mobility and which provided certain limited channels by which this mobility could be achieved. Since the approval of mobility *was* only limited, with the greater weight of sentiment in favor of fixed statuses, the bourgeoisie, as the only potentially mobile group in the society or at least the only group that could hope to cross from *roturier* to noble status, felt most acutely the strain of this ambivalence about mobility. It also had most to lose if those channels of mobility which enabled it to acquire nobility were threatened. Once the class system began to change in the direction of a caste society, in which statuses were predominantly hereditary and mobility was prohibited (and such a change did take place in the course of the century), this rigidification was felt as a blow particularly by the bourgeois and it may have made the strain on them intolerable.

The 18th century bourgeois was doubly the victim of the prevalent ambivalence in the matter of social mobility. First, he was the victim because he did have the necessary qualifications and attitudes for mobility. But second, and more important, the bourgeois *shared* in the predominant attitude of disapproval of mobility. His rational self-reliance as a competent man of business or lawyer did battle with his submissiveness to the traditional social and religious authorities. He hoped and expected to rise in the social scale, but he abandoned the "old" industrious and thrifty bourgeois way of life only with considerable hesitation and some feelings of moral delinquency. The bourgeois accepted the general definition of his business activities as worthy of contempt, but he denied the immutable inferiority of his position in the class structure. He accepted the superior dignity of the nobility, and even the hereditary character of this dignity, but he claimed, also, the right to attain this superior status for himself and his descendants.

The availability of adequate channels of mobility became a matter of great importance to the bourgeoisie. If 18th century French society had been a fully institutionalized caste system, the bourgeoisie would have accepted its inferior position as "just," and would have expected no change. As it was, however, the bourgeoisie had come to expect some approval of its achievements—not of the achievements per se, but as they provided the necessary means to adopt the noble way of life, both the functions and symbols of nobility. The availability of channels of mobility did not solve the conflict of values, but it mitigated it. In the course of the 18th century, the increasing restriction of the opportunities for mobility added the frustration of disappointment to the burden of moral conflict weighing on the bourgeois.

Among the important causes for the rigidification of the class structure was the reassertion by the nobility of its traditional rights, the so-called feudal reaction, which attempted to push the *roturier parvenu* back "where he belonged." The high *noblesse de robe* became a closed caste which venality of offices could no longer breach, and the *roturier* found himself excluded from officer status in the army. The nobility, which was largely self-excluded from the remunerative business field, tried increasingly to monopolize careers in the area of officialdom, in the army, and in the Church.[1] The disap-

[1] Dollot, *La question des privilèges*, p. 51.

pointed bourgeois, whose allegiance to the existing class system was, at best, in a state of tension, may well have felt, now, that this was an injustice that put too great a strain on his loyalty. The loosely established tradition that "each of the King's subjects, even if he was a *roturier*, had the right to cherish the highest hopes if his abilities were recognized," was being violated as a result of the "greed and intransigeance of the nobility [which] was to attain such magnitude that in 1788 there was to be found not a single *roturier* either in the government (with the exception of Necker) nor among the officers in the high grades, nor at the head of any dioceses."[2]

The pinch of the feudal reaction was felt differentially by the various elements within the bourgeoisie. This reaction, as we have suggested in an earlier chapter, owed its success, in part, to the fact that the French monarchy no longer had the strength to resist the demands of the nobility. And it follows therefrom that it was those channels of mobility through which the bourgeoisie was integrated into the noble class and which often depended on royal support, which could most easily be eliminated on the demand, or upon the unopposed action, of the aggressive nobility. The bourgeois who suffered most as a result of this shift in the internal balance of power were those of the middle bourgeoisie, who aimed at legal, political, military, or ecclesiastical careers, all of which integrated the mobile individual into the traditional class structure. Those bourgeois, on the other hand, whose social mobility was made possible by the assimilative power of great wealth or the uncontrollable asset of unusual genius were much less affected. It was very difficult, quite apart from being undesirable, to legislate either the great financiers or the leading intellectuals out of existence, or to bar them from the social contacts which their style of life, their wit, or their creativity opened to them.

To repeat, then, it was the middle bourgeoisie, chiefly, composed of merchants, manufacturers, lawyers, and doctors, that

2 *Ibid.*, p. 50.

was badly hit by the decrease in the opportunities for acquiring social prestige in general, and noble status in particular. And it was this group also which felt much more strongly than the financial and intellectual elite the conflict between traditional and new values and the strain of the normative inconsistencies in the French class system. Their increasing wealth, competence, and self-respect were far more serious sources of strain to them than they were to the financial elite, which simply used its wealth and power "for all they were worth." At best, the limited approval of mobility had caused difficulty in the definition of proper conduct and legitimate expectations on the part of these bourgeois. Now that the possibility of mobility was diminished yet further, these problematic and deeply important expectations were frustrated, and serious demoralization could easily result. It is our tentative suggestion, therefore, that it was the rigidification of the class system that precipitated the alienation of this segment of the bourgeoisie from the existing class structure to which it had, up to the Revolution, given its predominant allegiance. When he was denied the right to improve his social position, the bourgeois found the strain of conflicting moralities intolerable, so that he rejected altogether the disapproval of social mobility.

Strikingly enough, there were few expressions of egalitarian sentiments by bourgeois writers of the 18th century. The vast majority, as we have seen, supported the anti-egalitarian presuppositions of the structure of French society and of the French government. The bourgeois made no explicit assertions of the equal dignity of all men, nor of the equal right of all men to opportunity for advancement. Only implicitly did he claim for himself the right to change his inferior status to one that did have dignity; and once he became a nobleman, he tried to identify completely with his new social "equals." But when the limited opportunities for mobility were denied, he gradually swung over his predominant allegiance to the universalistic values on which his all-important claim to mobility depended.

Even in the *cahiers* of 1789, the demands for equality made by the Third Estate were "relative, . . . and almost never absolute."[3] The demands were made within the framework of the class system, and they took such forms as the demand for proportional taxation, which was unanimous, the demand for the abolition of class qualifications for officeholding, or, a demand stated in one fifth of the *cahiers* of the Third Estate, for equality before the law.[4] The Third Estate "present complete harmony in their desire for equality with the two upper orders," "but their motive was more frequently self-interest than the lofty ideal of equality."[5] As yet, they wanted only such things as political and fiscal equality; men like Siéyès demanded that the Third Estate, which contributed all that was of value to the nation, have its due share in government.

Egalitarian zeal was to go much further, though, before the Revolution was over, and among the circumstances that caused this wave of egalitarian sentiment, the rigidification of the class structure and its impact on the bourgeoisie may have played an important part. The bourgeoisie had become alienated from the old order which, in effect, had rejected its loyalty, and it tried to construct a new order in which its wealth and competence would be duly valued. The Jacobins devised many forms to symbolize social equality among men. For example, the universal appellation of "citoyen" and the abolition of clothes symbolizing class distinctions expressed the denial by the bourgeoisie of the traditional values that had betrayed them. It is true that revolutionary egalitarianism developed a momentum of its own, which, in the hands of proletarian extremists, threatened to go farther than the bourgeoisie wished, especially in the area of economic equality. But that part of the substance of the Revolution which consisted of the

---

[3] B. Hyslop, *French Nationalism in 1789 According to the General Cahier* (New York, 1934), p. 83.
    [4] *Ibid.*, pp. 84-86.
    [5] *Ibid.*, p. 89.

substitution, as the dominant ethos of French society, of universalistic and rational values for the particularistic and traditional values of the Old Regime made the bourgeois way of life the strategic one from then on. It represented the breakdown of the unstable class structure of 18th century France, and the triumph of the general approval of social mobility in which the bourgeoisie had such a large stake.

# BIBLIOGRAPHY*

## I. PRIMARY SOURCES

Bachaumont, Louis Petit de, *Anecdotes piquantes pour servir à l'histoire de la société française à la fin du règne de Louis XV*, Bruxelles, 1881

Barbier, Edmond J. F., *Chronique de la régence et du règne de Louis XV, 1718-1763*, 4v., Paris, 1857-75

————, *Journal historique et anecdotique du règne de Louis XV*, publié pour la Société de l'histoire de France d'après le manuscrit inédit de la Bibliothèque Royale par A. de Villegille, 4v., Paris, 1847-56

Beaumarchais, Pierre Augustin Caron de, *Les deux amis, ou le négociant de Lyon* (*Oeuvres complètes*, II), Paris, 1809

————, *La folle journée, ou le mariage de Figaro* (*Oeuvres complètes*, II), Paris, 1809

Berryer, *Souvenir de M. Berryer, doyen des avocats de Paris*, 2v., Paris, 1839

Besnard, F. Y., *Souvenirs d'un nonagénaire*, Paris, 1880

Boulaud, Joseph, ed., "Livre de raison de Grégoire Bénoist de Lostende (1677-1754)," *Bulletin de la Société archéologique et historique du Limousin*, LIX (1909), pp. 75-129

Campan, *Le mot et la chose*, s.l., 1751

Campan, Mme., *Mémoires sur la vie de Marie-Antoinette, reine de France et de Navarre; suivis de souvenirs et anecdotes historiques sur les règnes de Louis XIV, de Louis XV et de Louis XVI* (F. M. Barrière, ed., *Bibliothèque des mémoires relatifs à l'histoire de France pendant le 18e siècle*, X), Paris, 1849

Chérin, L. N. H., *La noblesse considérée sous divers rapports, dans les assemblées générales et particulières de la nation*, Paris, 1788

Chevrier, F. de, *Les ridicules du siècle*, Paris, 1752

Darigrand, Jean Baptiste, *L'antifinancier ou Relève de quelquesunes des malversations dont se rendent journellement coupables les Fermiers-Généraux, et des vexations qu'ils commettent dans les Provinces*, Amsterdam, 1763

---

* Some of the items in this bibliography are not specifically referred to in the text, but they are included here for the benefit of those wishing to pursue some aspect of this study further.

Duclos, Charles Pinot, *Considérations sur les moeurs de ce siècle*, Paris, 1881

———, *Mémoires sécrètes sur les règnes de Louis XIV et de Louis XV*, Paris, 1881

Dudevant, L. H., *L'apologie du commerce, essai philosophique et politique, avec des notes instructives: suivi de diverses reflexions sur le commerce en general, sur celui de la France en particulier, et sur les moyens propres à l'accroître et le perfectionner*. Par un jeune négociant, Genève, 1777

Epinay, Louise F. P. T. d'Esclavelles, Marquise d', *Mémoires*, Paul Boiteau, ed., 2v., Paris (1904?)

Garat, D. J. comte, *Mémoires historiques sur le 18e siècle, et sur M. Suard*, 2v., 2e édition, Paris, 1821

Garnier, Jean Jacques, *Le commerce remis à sa place; réponse d'un pédent de Collège aux novateurs politiques*, adressé à l'auteur de la lettre à M. F., 1756

Grosley, *Vie de M. Grosley*, Londres, 1787

Hanin, François, *Journal d'un bourgeois de Fécamp au 18e siècle*, publié par Alphonse Martin, Fécamp, 1887

Hardy, Siméon-Prosper, *Mes loisirs; journal d'évènements tels qu'ils parviennent à ma connaissance (1764-1789)* publié d'après le manuscrit autograph et inédit de la Bibliothèque nationale par Maurice Tourneux et Maurice Vitrac, Paris, 1912

Hervé-Bazin, "Récits inédits de François Chéron sur la vie de famille dans les classes bourgeoises avant la Révolution," *Revue de l'Anjou*, nouvelle série, II (1881), pp. 1-21, 65-87

La Bruyère, Jean de, *Les caractères, suivis des caractères de Theophraste, traduits du grec par le même*, Paris, 1824

Le Sage, A. M., *Turcaret*, E. E. Brandon et M. Baudoin, eds., N.Y., 1927

*Lettres de Madame Roland*, publiées par Claude Perroud, nouvelle série 1767-1780, 3v., Paris, 1913

Mairobert, Pidanzat de, *L'espion anglois ou correspondance sécrète entre Milord All'Eye et Milord All'Ear*, 10v. (Vol. I, pp. 1-275, *L'observateur hollandois à Paris*), Londres, 1784

Marais, Mathieu, *Journal et mémoires sur la régence et le règne de Louis XV (1715-1737)*, Paris, 1863-68

Marivaux, Pierre C. de Chamblain de, *L'île des esclaves (Oeuvres Complètes, v)*, Paris, 1781

———, *Le jeu de l'amour et du hasard (Théâtre complet de Marivaux*, J. Fournier et M. Bastide, eds., I), Paris, 1946

Marmontel, Jean-François, *Mémoires*, London, 1805

Mercier, Louis Sebastien, *Tableau de Paris*, nouvelle édition corrigée et augmentée, 12v., Amsterdam, 1783

Moreau, J. N., *Mes souvenirs*, 2v., Paris, 1898-1901

Morellet, Abbé, *Mémoires*, 2v., Paris, 1821

Narbonne, Pierre, *Journal des règnes de Louis XIV et Louis XV de l'anné 1701 à l'anné 1744*, Paris, 1866

Roland de la Platière, Marie Jeanne (Phlipon), *Mémoires* (*Oeuvres de J. M. Ph. Roland, femme de l'exministre de l'intérieure*, 1), 3v., Paris, an VIII (1800)

Savary, Jacques, *Le parfait négociant: ou Instruction générales pour ce qui regarde le commerce de tout sorte de marchandises, tant de France que de pays étrangers*, 2v., Paris, 1675

Sedaine, Michel Jean, *Félix* (*Oeuvres choisies de Sedaine*), Paris, 1903

————, *Le philosophe sans le savoir* (*Oeuvres choisies de Sedaine*), Paris, 1903

Ségur, Louis Philippe, Comte de, *Mémoires, souvenirs et anecdotes* (F. M. Barrière, ed., *Bibliothèque des mémoires relatifs à l'histoire de France pendant le 18e siècle*, XIX, XX), Paris, 1890

Sénac de Meilhan, Gabriel, *Considérations sur l'esprit et les moeurs*, London, 1787

————, *Considérations sur les richesses et le luxe*, Amsterdam, 1787

————, *Du gouvernement, des moeurs et des conditions en France avant la révolution, avec les caractères des principaux personnages du règne de Louis XVI*, Hamburg, 1795

Séras, P., *Le commerce ennobli*, Bruxelles, 1756

Tamizey de Larroque, Philippe, ed., "Livre de raison de la famille de Fontainemarie, 1640-1774," *Revue de l'Agenais et des anciennes provinces du Sud-Ouest. Bulletin de la Société des sciences, lettres et arts d'Agen*, XV, pp. 435-460, 494-526; XVI, pp. 93-116, 238-267, 322-360, 409-427

Thibaudeau, A. C., *Biographie, Mémoires 1765-92*, Paris, 1875

Tillette de Clermont Tonnerre, Adrien, ed., "Livre de raison d'un bourgeois d'Abbeville (Georges Mellier) (18e siècle)," *Bulletin de la Société d'émulation d'Abbeville*, V (1900-02), pp. 143, 189, 233

Voltaire, *Dictionnaire philosophique* (*Oeuvres Complètes*, XXIX-XXXII), Paris, 1819

Voltaire, *Le droit du seigneur*, comédie (*Oeuvres de Voltaire*, VI), Paris, 1838

————, *La femme qui a raison*, comédie (*Oeuvres de Voltaire*, IV), Paris, 1838

————, *Nanine, ou le préjugé vaincu* (*Oeuvres de Voltaire*, IV), Paris, 1838

Young, Arthur, *Travels in France and Italy during the Years 1787, 1788, and 1789*, London, New York, 1915?

## II. SECONDARY WORKS

Accarias, Joseph, "Un publiciste dauphinois au 18e siècle: Jacques Accarias de Sérionne, sa famille, sa vie et ses ouvrages," *Bulletin de l'Académie delphinale*, 4e série, III (1889), pp. 487-533

Ageorges, Joseph, *La vie et l'organisation du clergé sous l'ancien régime*, 2v., Paris, 1905

Ardashev, Paul, *L'administration provinciale en France, 1774-1789*, Paris, 1909

Artaud, Adrien, "Georges Roux, Etudes historiques sur le 18e siècle," *Revue de Marseilles* XXXI (1885), pp. 449-460; XXXII (1886), pp. 11-32, 109-128, 312-335, 413-442, 522-542; XXXIII (1887), pp. 127-155, 245-282, 412-436, 500-507; XXXIV (1888), pp. 5-28, 68-74, 114-141, 227-238, 249-259, 339-355, 446-466

Aynard, Joseph, *La bourgeoisie française; essai de psychologie*, Paris, 1924

Babeau, Albert, *Les bourgeois d'autrefois*, Paris, 1886

————, *La province sous l'ancien régime*, Paris, 1894

————, *La vie militaire sous l'ancien régime*, 2v., Paris, 1890

————, *La ville sous l'ancien régime*, Paris, 1880

Barber, Bernard, " 'Mass Apathy' and Voluntary Participation in the United States," unpublished Ph.D. thesis, Harvard University, 1949

————, and Lyle Lobel, " 'Fashion' in Women's Clothes and the American Social System," *Social Forces*, XXXI (Dec. 1952), pp. 124-131

Bastard d'Estaing, Henry B., vicomte de, *Les parlements de France; essai historique sur leurs usages, leurs organisations, et leur autorité*, 2v., Paris, 1858

Baudrillart, Henri, *Histoire du luxe privé et public depuis l'an-tiquité jusqu'à nos jours*, 4v., Paris, 1878-80

Bayle, Paul, et A. Fauchier-Magnan, "Pierre Crozat, un curieux sous la Régence," *Nouvelle Revue*, 6e série, XXXII (1905), pp. 163-187

Beaune, H., "Les avocats d'autrefois," *La réforme sociale*, 2e série, I (janvier, 1886)

Becker, Carl, *The Heavenly City of the 18th Century Philos-ophers*, New Haven, 1932

Bénoist, Charles, "La hiérarchie des professions dans l'ancienne so-ciété française," *Séances et travaux de l'Académie des sci-ences morales*. Compte rendu (Paris), CLXXV (1911), pp. 98-110

Bernard, Maurice, *La municipalité de Brest de 1750 à 1790*, Paris, 1915

Bertin, Ernest, *Les mariages dans l'ancien société française, particu-lièrement après les mémoires de Saint-Simon*, Paris, 1879

Beylié, Jules de, "Barnave avocat," *Bulletin de l'Académie delphi-nale*, 5e série, IX (1914-1917), pp. 137-262

Brocher, H., *Le rang et l'etiquette sous l'ancien régime*, Le Mans, 1936

Bouchard, Marcel, *L'évolution des esprits dans la bourgeoisie bour-guignonne*, Paris, 1929

Bouchary, Jean, "Un manieur d'argent avant la Révolution fran-çaise. Etienne Clavière, d'après sa correspondance financière et politique," *Revue d'histoire économique et politique*, XXIV (1938), pp. 131-162

Boulloche, P., *Un avocat au 18e siècle: Target*, Paris, 1893

Bourde de la Rogerie, H., *Introduction à l'inventaire sommaire des archives départmentales antérieures à 1790. Finistère*, Archives civiles, Série B, III

Brace, Richard M., *Bordeaux and the Gironde, 1789-91*, Ithaca, 1947

Braure, Maurice, *Lille et la Flandre wallonne au 18e siècle*, 2v., Lille, 1932

Burrell, Sidney A., "Kirk, Crown and Covenant," unpublished Ph.D. thesis, Columbia University, 1953

Bussière, Georges, *Etudes historiques sur la révolution en Péri-gord*, 2v. (Vol. I, *La bourgeoisie périgourdienne au 18e siècle*), Bordeaux, 1877-1903

Butterfield, Herbert, *The Origins of Modern Science, 1300-1800*, London, 1949

Caix de Saint-Aymon, *Une famille d'artiste et de financiers du 17e et 18e siècle. Les Boullongnes,* Paris, 1914

Capefigue, J. B. H. R., *Louis XV et la société du 18e siècle,* 4v. (I-III, v), Bruxelles, 1842

Cardevacque, Achille de, "Essai sur la bourgeoisie d'Arras avant la Révolution de 1789," *Mémoires de l'Académie d'Arras,* 2e série, XIX (1886), pp. 195-224

Carré, Henri, *La fin des parlements (1788-90),* Paris, 1912

————, *La France sous Louis XV,* Paris, 1891

————, *La noblesse de France et l'opinion publique au 18e siècle,* Paris, 1920

————, *Le règne de Louis XV, 1715-1774* (E. Lavisse, ed., *Histoire de France,* VIII, part 2), Paris, 1909

Chérel, Albert, *De Télémaque à Candide,* Paris, 1933

Chevalier, Jean, *Le Creusot, berceau de la grande industrie française,* Paris, Bruxelles, 1946

Clément, Pierre, et A. Lemoine, *M. de Silhouette, Bouret et les derniers fermiers généraux; études sur les financiers du 18e siècle,* Paris, 1872

Clermont-Tonnerre, E., *Histoire de Samuel Bernard et de ses enfants,* Paris, 1914

Coornaert, Emile, *Les corporations en France avant 1789,* Paris, 1941

Cucuel, G., "La vie de société dans le Dauphinois au 18e siècle," *Revue d'histoire littéraire de la France,* XLII (1935), pp. 44-74

Davis, Kingsley, and Wilbert E. Moore, "Some Principles of Stratification," *American Sociological Review,* X (April, 1945)

Delacroix, Abbé Alphonse E., *M. de Boulogne, archévêque-évêque de Troyes,* Paris, 1886

Delahante, A., *Une famille de finance au 18e siècle,* Paris, 1881

Delbèke, Baron Francis, *L'action politique et sociale des avocats au 18e siècle. Leur part dans la préparation de la Révolution française,* Louvain, 1927

Demartial, André, "Achat d'une charge de sécrétaire du Roi par Jacques Pétiniaud de Beaupeyrat en 1779," *Bulletin de la Société archéologique et historique du Limousin,* LIX (1909), pp. 67-74

Dépitre, Egard, "Le système et la querelle de la Noblesse commerçante (1756-1759)," *Revue d'histoire économique et sociale,* 6e année (1913), pp. 137-176

Desdevises du Dezert, D., "L'église et l'état en France, depuis l'Edit de Nantes jusqu'à nos jours. L'église au 18e siècle," *Revue des cours et conférences*, XIV² (1906), pp. 210-225

Desnoiresterres, Gustave, *La comédie satirique au 18e siècle. Histoire de la société française par allusion, par personalité et la satire au théâtre, Louis XV, Louis XVI, et la Revolution*, Paris, 1885

————, *Grimod de la Reynière et son groupe*, Paris, 1877

Dollot, Louis, *La question des privilèges dans la seconde moitié du 18e siècle*, Paris, 1941

du Boys, Albert, "Notice sur Barthelémy d'Orbanne," *Bulletin de l'Académie delphinale*, 3e série, I (1865), pp. 409-434

Ducéré, E., "La bourgeoisie bayonnaise sous l'ancien régime," *Bulletin de la Société des sciences, lettres et arts de Pau*, 2e série, XVIII (1888-89), pp. 87-255

Ducourtieux, Paul, "Les Barbou, imprimeurs. Lyon-Limoges-Paris. 1524-1893," *Bulletin de la Société archéologique et historique du Limousin*, XLI (1894), pp. 121-208; XLII (1894), pp. 187-225; XLIII (1895), pp. 361-504; XLIV (1896), pp. 77-178

Ducros, Louis, *La société française au 18e siècle*, d'après les mémoires et les correspondances du temps, Paris, 1922

Dumoulin, Maurice, "Les livres de raison," *Revue de Paris*, III (1901), pp. 404-430

Duruy, Albert, *L'armée royale en 1789*, Paris, 1888

Egret, Jean, "L'aristocratie parlementaire française à la fin de l'ancien régime," *Revue historique*, CCVIII (July-Sept. 1952), pp. 1-15

————, *Le Parlement de Dauphiné et les affaires publiques dans la deuxième moitié du 18e siècle*, 2v., Grenoble, Paris, 1942

Fage, René, *La vie à Tulle aux 17e et 18e siècles*, Paris, 1902

Fontaine, Léon, *Le théâtre et la philosophie au 18e siècle*, Versailles, 1878

Ford, Franklin L., *Robe and Sword. The Regrouping of the French Aristocracy after Louis XIV*, Cambridge, Mass., 1953

Foster, Charles A., "Honoring Commerce and Industry in 18th Century France; a Case Study of Changes in Traditional Social Functions," unpublished Ph.D. thesis, Harvard University, 1950

Fouquier, Henri, "Le théâtre de Sedaine—'Le philosophe sans le savoir,' " *Revue des cours et conférences*, VII (1899), pp. 599-608

Froment, Théodore, "Un salon parlementaire à Bordeaux au 18e siècle," *Revue philomatique de Bordeaux et du Sud-Ouest,* I (1897), pp. 113-133

Gaffiot, Maurice, "La théorie du luxe dans l'oeuvre de Voltaire," *Revue d'histoire économique et sociale,* XIV (1926), pp. 320-343

Gaiffe, Félix, *Etude sur le drame en France au 18e siècle,* Paris, 1910

Gaudry, Joachim Antoine Joseph, *Histoire du barreau de Paris depuis son origine jusqu'à 1830,* 2v., Paris, 1864

Garnault, Emile, "Les bourgeois rochelais des temps passés et les causes de la décadence du commerce rochelais," *Revue historique,* LXX (1899), pp. 53-67

————, *Le commerce rochelais au 18e siècle,* 2v. (Vol. I, *La réprésentation commerciale de La Rochelle*), La Rochelle, 1888

Gill-Mark, Grace, *Une femme de lettres au 18e siècle. Anne-Marie Du Boccage,* Paris, 1927

Glotz, Marguerite, *Salons du 18e siècle,* Paris, 1945

Goehring, Martin, *Die Aemterkaeuflichkeit im Ancien Regime,* Berlin, 1938

————, *Geschichte der Grossen Revolution,* 2v. (Vol. I, *Sturz des Ancien Regime und Sieg der Revolution*), Tuebingen, 1950

————, *Weg und Sieg der modernen Staatsidee in Frankreich vom Mittelalter zu 1789,* Tuebingen, 1946

Goldschmidt, W. R., "America's Social Classes," *Commentary,* X (August, 1950), pp. 175-181

Green, Frederick Charles, *French Novelists, Manners and Ideas from the Renaissance to the Revolution,* London, Toronto, 1929?

————, *La peinture des moeurs de la bonne société dans le roman français de 1715 à 1761,* Paris, 1924

Groethuysen, Bernhard, *Die Entstehung der Buergerlichen Welt- und Lebensanschauung in Frankreich,* 2v., Halle, 1927-30

————, *Origines de l'esprit bourgeois en France,* Paris, 1927

Guéneau, Louis, *Les conditions de la vie à Nevers à la fin de l'ancien régime,* Paris, 1919

Hartman, Louis, "Les officiers de l'armée royale à la veille de la Révolution," *Revue historique,* C (1900), pp. 241-268; CI (1901), pp. 38-79

Hauser, Henri, "Le 'Parfait Négociant' de Jacques Savary," *Revue d'histoire économique et sociale*, XIII (1925), pp. 1-28

Heilman, Eleonore, *Charles Pinot Duclos, Ein Literat des 18ten Jahrhunderts, und seine Beziehungen zu Rousseau, d'Alembert, Marmontel und anderen*, Wuerzburg, 1936

Hennet, L., *Les milices et les troupes provinciales*, Paris, 1884

Hermant, Abel, *Le bourgeois*, Paris, 1924

Hocquart de Turtot, E., *Le tiers état et les privilèges*, Paris, 1907

Honigsheim, Paul, *Staats und Soziallehren der Franzoesischen Jansenisten im 17ten Jahrhundert*, Heidelberg, 1914

Janzé, Alix de, *Les financiers d'autrefois; fermiers généraux*, Paris (cover, 1886)

Joubert, André, "Les fermes générales depuis leur institution jusqu'à la Révolution française," *Revue de l'Anjou*, nouvelle série, II (1880), pp. 355-383

Kolabinska, Marie, *La circulation des élites en France, Etude historique depuis la fin du 11e siècle jusqu'à la Grande Révolution*, Lausanne, 1912

Kowalewsky, Maksim M., *La France économique et sociale à la veille de la Révolution*, 2v., Paris, 1909-1914

Lacroix, Paul, *18e siècle, institutions, usages et coûtumes; France 1700-1789*, Paris, 1875

La Gorce, Pierre de, *Histoire réligieuse de la Révolution française*, Paris, 1917

Lamy, Etienne (Ed.), *Un défenseur des principes traditionnels sous la Révolution. Nicolas Bergasse. Avocat au Parlement de Paris. Député du tiers état de la sénéchaussée de Lyon aux Etats-Généraux (1750-1832)*, Paris, 1910

Landes, David S., "French Entrepreneurship and Industrial Growth in the 19th Century," *Journal of Economic History*, IX (May 1949)

Lapouyade, Méaudre de, "Les Dirouard, bourgeois et marchands de Bordeaux," *Revue historique de Bordeaux*, XXI, pp. 161-176, 217-236; XXII, pp. 3040, 7090

Latreille, Albert, *L'armée et la nation à la fin de l'ancien régime, les derniers ministres de la guerre de la monarchie*, Paris, 1914

Lefèbvre, Georges, *The Coming of the French Revolution*, R. R. Palmer, transl., Princeton, 1947

Legros, Adrien, "Les dépenses d'un bourgeois de Valenciennes à la veille de la Révolution," *Revue du Nord*, VIII (1922), pp. 210-225, 253-278

Le Lay, F., *Histoire de la ville et communauté de Ponthivy au 18e siècle*, Paris, 1911

Leroux, Alfred, *Etude critique sur le 18e siècle à Bordeaux*, Bordeaux, 1921

Leuilliot, P., "Reflexions sur l'histoire économique et sociale à propos de la bourgeoisie de 1789," *Revue d'histoire moderne et contemporaine*, I (1954), pp. 131-144

Lévy-Bruhl, Henri, "La noblesse de France et le commerce à la fin de l'ancien régime," *Revue d'histoire moderne*, VIII (1923), pp. 211ff.

Lockit, C. H., *The Relations of French and English Society (1763-1793)*, London, 1920

Low, D. M., *Edward Gibbon, 1737-1794*, London, 1937

Mallortie, H. de, "Discours d'ouverture: Un salon au 18e siècle —Madame Geoffrin," *Mémoires de l'Académie d'Arras*, 2e série, XXIII (1892), pp. 9-32

Marion, Marcel, *Dictionnaire des institutions de la France au 17e et 18e siècle*, Paris, 1923

————, *Histoire financière de la France depuis 1715*, 6v., Paris, 1914-1931

Martin, Germain, *La grande industrie sous le règne de Louis XV*, Paris, 1900

Masson, F., *L'Académie Française, 1629-1793*, Paris, 1912

Maupassant, Jean de, "Les armateurs bordelais au 18e siècle. Abraham Gradis et l'approvisionnement des colonies (1756-63)," *Revue historique de Bordeaux*, II (1909), pp. 174-195, 248-265

————, "Un grand armateur de Bordeaux. Abraham Gradis. (1699?-1780)," *Revue historique de Bordeaux*, VI (1913), pp. 175-196, 276-297, 344-367, 423-448; VII (1913), pp. 53-67, 118-139, 272-289, 329-345

Mention, Léon, *L'armée de l'ancien régime de Louis XIV à la Révolution*, Paris, 1900

Merton, Robert K., *Social Theory and Social Structure, Toward the Codification of Theory and Research*, Glencoe, Illinois, 1949

Morazé, Charles, *La France bourgeoise, 18e-20e siècles*, preface de L. Fèbvre, Paris, 1946

Morize, André, *L'apologie du luxe au 18e siècle et "Le Mondain" de Voltaire*, Paris, 1909

Mornet, D., "La vie mondaine, les salons," *La vie parisienne au 18e siècle*, Leçons faites à l'école des hautes études sociales, Paris, 1914

————, *Les origines intellectuelles de la Révolution française (1715-1787)*, Paris, 1933

Mousnier, Roland, *La vénalité des offices sous Henri IV et Louis XIII*, Rouen, 1945

Olivier, Léopold, "Les Déroulède sous l'ancien régime. Essai de réconstitution d'un livre de raison," *Souvenirs et mémoires*, IV (1900), pp. 1-28, 117-141

Olivier-Martin, F. J. M., *L'organisation corporative de la France de l'ancien régime*, Paris, 1938

Pagès, G., "La vénalité des offices dans l'ancienne France," *Revue historique*, CLXIX (1932), pp. 477-495

Parsons, Talcott, *Essays in Sociological Theory, Pure and Applied*, Glencoe, Illinois, 1948

Peirce, Walter T., *The Bourgeois from Molière to Beaumarchais: the Study of a Dramatic Type*, Columbus, Ohio, 1907

Perey, Lucien, et Gaston Maugras, *Une femme du monde au 18e siècle, la jeunesse de Madame d'Epinay*, Paris, 1882

Picard, Roger, *Les salons littéraire et la société française (1610-1789)*, New York, 1943

Pilon, Edmond, *La vie de famille au 18e siècle*, Paris, 1923

Rébillon, Armand, "Recherches sur les anciennes corporations ouvrières et marchandes de la ville de Rennes," *Annales de Bretagne* (1902), pp. 1-48

Rémond, André, *John Holker, manufacturier et grand fonctionnaire en France au 18e siècle, 1719-1786*, Paris, 1946

Ribbe, Charles de, *Les familles et la société française avant la Révolution*, 2v., Paris, 1874

————, *La vie domestique, ses modèles et ses règles d'après des documents originaux*, 2v., Paris, 1877-78

Richard, Jules-Marie, *La vie privée dans une province de l'Ouest: Laval au 17e et 18e siècle*, Paris, 1922

Robbe, Marie-Agnès, "La milice dans l'intendance de la Flandre wallonne au 18e siècle," *Revue du Nord*, XXIII (1937), pp. 5-50

Robin, Pierre, *La compagnie des secrétaires du roi (1351-1791)*, Paris, 1933

Robison, Georgia, *Revelliere-Lepeaux, Citizen-Director, 1753-1824*, New York, 1938

Rouff, Marcel, *Les mines de charbon au 18e siècle, 1744-91*, Paris, 1922

———, *Tubeuf, un grand industriel français au 18e siècle*, Paris, 1922

Roupnel, Gaston, *Les populations de la ville et de la compagne dijonnaise au 17e siècle*, Paris, 1922

Roustan, Marius, *Les philosophes et la société française au 18e siècle*, Lyon, 1906

Roux, Marquis de, *La Révolution à Poitiers et dans la Vienne* (*Mémoires de la Société des antiquaires de l'Ouest*, 3e série, IV [1910], pp. 1-589)

Royer, Louis, et H. Chobaut, "La famille maternelle de Stendhal: Les Gagnon," *Revue d'histoire littéraire de la France*, XLI (1937), pp. 189-207

Ruhlmann, Georges, *Les corporations, les manufactures et le travail à Abbeville au 18e siècle*, Préface d'Emile Coornaert, Paris, 1948

Sagnac, Philippe, *Formation de la société française moderne*, 2v., Paris, 1945-46

Saulnier, Frédéric, "Le barreau du Parlement de Bretagne au 18e siècle (1733-89)," *Revue des provinces de l'Ouest*, 8e livraison (Avril 1856), p. 484

Sée, Henri, "Les armateurs de Saint-Malo au 18e siècle," *Revue d'histoire économique et sociale*, XVII (1929), pp. 29-35

———, "Dans quelle mésure puritains et juifs ont-ils contribué au progrès du capitalisme moderne?" *Revue historique*, CLV (1927), pp. 57-68

———, *L'évolution commerciale et industrielle de la France sous l'ancien régime*, Paris, 1925

———, *Histoire économique de la France*, 2v. (Vol. I, *Le moyen age et l'ancien régime*), Paris, 1939

———, "Le rôle de la bourgeoisie bretonne à la veille de la Révolution," *Annales de Bretagne*, XXXIV (1919-1920), pp. 405-433

———, *La vie économique et les classes sociales en France au 18e siècle*, Paris, 1924

Sicard, Abbé, *L'ancien clergé de France*, 2v. (Vol. I, *Les évêques avant la Révolution*), Paris, 1899-1905

Sombart, Werner, *Le bourgeois. Contribution à l'histoire morale et intellectuelle de l'homme économique moderne*, Paris, 1926

———, *Luxury and Capitalism*, New York, 1938

———, *Der Moderne Kapitalismus*, 2v., Leipzig, 1902

Sorel, Albert, "La vie de famille au 18e siècle," *La vie parisienne au 18e siècle*, conférences du Musée Carnavalet (1928), Paris, 1928

Teissier, Octave, "Les échevins Georges Roux et Justinien de Rémuzat. Etude sur la constitution municipale de la ville de Marseilles pendant le 18e siècle," *Revue de Marseilles*, xx (1874), pp. 569-573; xxi (1875), pp. 97-111

————, *La maison d'un bourgeois au 18e siècle*, Paris, 1886

Thirion, Henri, *La vie privée des financiers au 18e siècle*, Paris, 1895

Thomas, Louis J., *Montpellier, ville marchande*, Montpellier, 1936

Tocqueville, Alexis de, *The Old Regime and the Revolution*, John Bonner, transl., New York, 1856

Toublet, Abbé E., "Un industriel au 18e siècle. Elie Savatier," *Revue historique et archéologique du Maine*, xlvi (1899), pp. 34-47, 197-208, 246-260; xlvii (1900), pp. 82-110

Trinterude, Leonard J., "The Origins of Puritanism," *Church History*, xx (March 1951), pp. 37-57

Tronchin, Henri, *Un médecin au 18e siècle. Théodore Tronchin (1709-1781)*, Paris, 1906

Tuetey, Louis, *Les officiers sous l'ancien régime. Nobles et roturiers*, Paris, 1908

Vaissière, Pierre de, "L'état sociale des curés de campagne au 18e siècle," *Revue de l'histoire de l'église de France*, xix (1923), pp. 23-53

Vanel, G., *Une grande ville au 17e et 18e siècle. La vie publique à Caen. Moeurs et coûtumes*, Caen, 1910

Vavasseur, A., "La bourgeoisie dans le passé," *Revue des études historiques*, lxiii (1897), pp. 14-35

Vermale, F., "Les années de jeunesse de Mounier (1758-1787)," *Annales historiques de la Révolution française*, xvi (1939), pp. 1-24

Weber, Max, *The Protestant Ethic and the Spirit of Capitalism*, T. Parsons, transl., New York, 1930

Wilkinson, Spenser, *The French Army before Napoleon*, Oxford, 1915

Wolff, Louis, *Le Parlement de Provence au 18e siècle*, Aix-en-Provence, 1920

# INDEX